IT FREE
FALL

THE BUSINESS OWNER'S GUIDE TO AVOIDING TECHNOLOGY PITFALLS

by

Nick Bernfeld & Paul Riendeau

This book is dedicated to the clients of SNECS, LLC.

Thank you for giving us the honor and privilege of serving you.

Table of Contents

INTRODUCTION

TECHNOLOGY IS BECOMING MORE COMPLICATED? CAN YOU KEEP UP?

Photo by Torkild Retvedt

INTRODUCTION

It doesn't matter if you are at the helm of a growing business with lots of employees or if you proudly own a small "Mom and Pop" operation, every modern business needs technology to function. From payment processing to marketing and advertising to accounting, every business in existence today relies on at least some level of technology to conduct daily business operations.

When everything is working properly, this increased dependence on technology is a good thing. Computers and related technology provide your business with numerous advantages including increased productivity, better customer service, and accurate reporting that can be used to plan for the future.

But what happens when this technology doesn't work? This is the downside of technology, and it can be frustrating at the very least. In extreme cases of technology failure, an entire business can be destroyed overnight. Whether it's a temporary setback or a major disaster, a technology failure is a serious concern -- or at least it should be. Lost revenue, a decreasing customer base, and a host of other issues can all result from even a relatively small network outage lasting only a few hours.

It's Not a Matter Of If, But When, Technology Fails

No business is immune from computer problems and failures. Sure, that fancy new machine you just bought may work well with no maintenance for the first month or two of service, but what happens when that shiny new machine gets a virus, needs a critical security update, or crashes randomly for no apparent reason? What if that machine is essential to your business? Think payment processing, monitoring inventory, order taking, payroll, etc… The list of business-critical processes that could be affected by a technology failure is endless, but the consequences are almost always the same.

And don't forget about the complexity of installing new equipment in the first place. What do you buy? How will these new purchases integrate with existing hardware and software? It's OK if you don't know the answers to these questions. The reality is that most business owners don't. After all, you're worried about maintaining and growing your business, not the latest trends in wireless access points, solid state hard drives, and how many terabytes of data storage you need to store important customer data, right?

While it's true that many small business owners are forced to wear many hats, staying on top of

INTRODUCTION

technology trends and understanding the nuances of network maintenance is a job best left to the professionals.

The costs of not taking Information Technology (**IT**) seriously can be astronomical. Although you will learn much more about how expensive poor IT management can be in Chapter One, businesses have gone bankrupt practically overnight because of catastrophic data loss. These horror stories happen all the time and what's even worse is that most of them could have been avoided had the business spent more time properly managing the technology responsible for the failure.

And let's not forget about the growing concerns surrounding the security of your business technology. There are hackers around the world that would simply love to gain access to your network and use your business and customer data for many nefarious purposes. One only needs to peruse the news headlines to find countless stories of businesses large and small that have been victimized by hackers. Major retailers including Target, Neiman Marcus, Home Depot, and Adobe have all fallen victim to embarrassing and expensive security breaches in just the last year. If these large companies are susceptible to attack, what makes you think your business isn't as well? The difference is that your Small to Mid-Sized

INTRODUCTION

Business (**SMB**) may not have deep enough pockets to recover from such a catastrophic breach. In the Target breach, for example, the payment information for over 40 million customers was compromised. Could your business recover from a similar disaster? In most cases, the answer is "nope, not a chance."

Network security is a whole separate issue and also something that should be left to those people who have been trained to deal with the many security threats that the SMB faces. You will learn about some of these threats later in this book (some of them are scary).

This book has been divided into two parts. The first part is written to help you realize the importance of hiring professional IT support to help manage your business's technology. More than that, it teaches you how to find the best IT support in a market crowded with incompetent (yet often well-meaning) technicians that can actually cause more harm than good.

In Part I, you will learn the answers to some of these common questions:

- How do you ensure that the investments you make in technology (both hardware and software) are actually working to support your business goals while interoperating the way they should?

- How do you avoid the "latest and greatest" trends while investing in technology that offers a legitimate competitive advantage?
- How do you protect your business data from hackers, malware, faulty equipment, and even your own employees?

The short answer to all of these questions is hiring a competent, reliable IT consultant who takes the time to understand your business and is capable of making sound recommendations that reflect your current and future business goals.

You will learn exactly how to find such a person – a business partner if you will – in the chapters that follow. Not only that, you will also learn how to maximize the relationship with your IT consultant to practically guarantee that your business technology becomes a quantifiable business asset rather than an expensive and time-consuming liability that leads to nothing but frustration and lost business earnings.

In Part II, you will learn how to protect your business from security threats. Although not meant to be an all-inclusive "how-to" guide, Part II highlights the importance of remaining a proactive part of network maintenance and security.

INTRODUCTION

You will learn why this is important in the first part of this book and what your responsibilities as a business owner should be when it comes to the technology behind your business processes.

Don't worry -- you need not understand a bunch of 'geek speak' to effectively manage your network and the IT professionals you hire to do the work -- a basic understanding of technology best practices will be more than enough to put you well ahead of most SMB owners (including your competition) in business today.

Why Finding a Competent Computer Consultant Isn't As Easy As a Quick Google Search

You've probably heard plenty of horror stories related to substandard IT work ranging from minor inconveniences to outright catastrophes that could cost thousands to fix (if you're lucky). If you've been in business for any amount of time, you may have even experienced some of these issues personally. The reason stories like this abound can be simplified into a single reason is this: lack of regulation.

Unlike many other professional fields (think lawyers, accountants, doctors, realtors, etc.) the computer industry is still in its infancy. This means there is little to no regulation concerning IT support. Anybody can open a computer repair business and although these people may have the best of intentions, without the proper knowledge and experience to get the job done right the first time, you could pay way too much, suffer poor network performance, or even lose all of your valuable business data in the blink of an eye (just to name a few).

Even though there isn't enough regulation to protect your business from intentionally unethical computer consultants, the good news is that few people are out to rip you off on purpose. The bigger problem, and one you are likely to encounter if you're not vigilant, is the well-meaning, but entirely incompetent, computer technician. These people want to do right by you and try their best to deliver quality service at an affordable price, but, unfortunately, the reality often falls far short of the ideal.

Inexperienced technicians can cost you a fortune in additional time and resources as they try to figure out how to best meet your business's needs. An experienced consultant, on the other hand, will already know what works and doesn't work. This means you aren't paying for solutions that could meet your needs or might work for your business.

INTRODUCTION

But there's no need to worry. The fact that you're reading this book means you will be well-equipped to sort out these incompetent individuals by the time you finish. You will know exactly what questions to ask of a potential IT consultant to ensure that this person (or people) is well-equipped to meet the needs of your business now and well into the future.

In summary, here's what you can expect to learn from this book:

- How to become an educated buyer of IT support services.
- How to avoid spending excessive time and money working with incompetent or unethical consultants.
- Learn to reduce overall IT costs without sacrificing performance or reliability
- Secure your business network from malware, hackers, natural disasters, and data loss.
- Eliminating computer problems that waste time and cause frustration.
- Turn technology into a competitive advantage, not a drain of time, money and resources.

It's a lot of information to cover, but this book has been designed to make it easy to learn. Each

INTRODUCTION

chapter covers a distinct part of this process and has been written in a way you can understand whether you already know something about the technology your business relies on or if you really have no clue. In Chapter One, for instance, you will learn about the hidden costs associated with choosing the wrong IT support company. Once you learn just how expensive it can be, you'll wonder why you waited so long to find the right company to handle your business technology.

CHAPTER ONE

THE INVISIBLE COSTS OF CHOOSING THE WRONG IT COMPANY

Photo by TaxRebate.org.uk

CHAPTER ONE

Just about everyone can relate on some level to the frustration that can be caused by computer problems. From system crashes to latency issues to the printer that just never seems to work right, there is no shortage of reasons why technology can make you want to pull your hair out without a moment's hesitation.

These problems present themselves at the consumer level (i.e. home computers used for personal reasons) and at the business level. All technology, no matter how expensive or 'state-of-the-art', is susceptible to issues and while most of us can relate to the frustration these problems cause when they arise, very few business owners ever put a dollar figure on these costs.

Why does this occur?

Simply put, while it's easy to put a dollar amount to the cost of a new server, network switch, or wireless access point (these are all physical goods with a set purchase and installation price), it's not so easy to put a dollar amount to the soft costs of IT equipment. Primarily, these soft costs include decreased productivity, more hours worked, and time lost trying to figure out these technology headaches when they occur. Of course, that doesn't even take into account abstract costs such as customer churn that may be directly related to technology failures that could have been avoided with proper configuration and maintenance.

Statistics That Should Frighten You

Did you know that the average cost of network downtime per year has increased every year for the last five years? From 2010 to 2012, for instance, the cost of downtime per year has increased from $98,000 to $138,000 (Aberdeen Group), and these numbers continue to increase at any alarming rate.

Small and mid-sized businesses are affected the most by these network events. Consider these figures taken from the same Aberdeen Group study:

A small business of less than 100 employees experiences, on average, 1.7 downtime events per year. The average length of each event is 2.2 hours, and the cost of this downtime averages $6,900 per hour. That's the equivalent of $25,806 in lost income each year.

Mid-sized businesses (100 to 1000 employees) are hit even harder. The average mid-sized business will experience 3.5 network downtime events each year. The length of each event is approximately 3.4 hours and the cost per hour for each event is a whopping $74,000. That equals close to $900,000 per year in lost revenue stemming from network downtime events that could have been avoided (or at least significantly reduced) with proper network management.

Another study, conducted by Gartner, projected that through 2015, 80% of all unplanned IT outages will be caused by people and process issues. In other words, poor IT management (whether intentional or accidental) will cause outages for SMBs that could cost up to a million dollars in lost revenue each year.

A USA Today survey of 200 data center managers found that over 80% of these managers reported that downtime costs exceeded $50,000 per hour. Even if your business is relatively small, can you really afford the lost revenue associated with even an hour of downtime? For most SMB owners, the answer is a definite no.

It's common for a business owner to think "Oh...that won't happen to me" but did you know that 20% of SMBs will suffer a major IT disaster resulting in catastrophic loss of critical data every five years? (Richmond House Group). Over a long enough time line, that means just about every SMB will suffer catastrophic data failure unless steps are taken to mitigate the risks associated with poor network maintenance and management. And it gets worse because 93% of all companies (large and small) that lost their data center for 10 days or more due to an IT disaster filed for bankruptcy within one year. Of those, 50% filed for bankruptcy immediately following the disaster.

Here's an example of a company who narrowly missed going bankrupt following a severe network outage: In September 2010, Virgin Blue's airline check-in and online booking systems suffered a catastrophic hardware failure that resulted in an 11-day outage. In total, this outage affected approximately 50,000 passengers and over 400 flights. Estimated financial losses during this outage were around $20 million for Virgin Blue. The only reason the company was able to stay afloat was because Navitaire, the company in charge of the reservation system, compensated Virgin Blue for this lost revenue. Virgin Blue was lucky, but would anyone bail out your business if it suffered a similar fate? For most SMBs, there is no bailout when network technology fails. You lose revenue, customers, and market share overnight. In many cases, the business cannot survive this series of events, and the sad thing is that most of these catastrophic IT failures could have been avoided with regular maintenance performed by a competent IT consultant.

And if the thought of a hardware or software failure bringing your business to its knees isn't enough, also consider the ever increasing threat of hackers to your business technology assets. According to a Gartner Group study, cybercriminals have stolen an average of $900 from each of 3 million Americans in the past year. Can your business afford to hemorrhage money due to poor network security? Not to mention the affect that cybercrime could have on your customers.

Just last year, the payment information for over 40 million Target customers was compromised due to a simple oversight within the IT department that allowed hackers to install malware on a Point of Sale (**POS**) terminal. Keep in mind that Target has a large in-house IT department and even it wasn't able to stop this breach. How easy do you think it would be for hackers to access a network not currently supported by a professional IT staff? 'Not hard at all' would be an understatement.

How Much Does Bad Advice Actually Cost Your Business?

The statistics above are meant to highlight some of the costs associated with improperly managed networks, but there is another cost that the SMB owner needs to be aware of. That is the cost of bad advice. Usually, bad advice stems from an inexperienced IT consultant who recommends products, services, or projects that are either unnecessary or incorrect for your business.

Inexperienced consultants may not take into consideration the hidden costs of a project he or she is recommending, or they may underestimate the actual time and money it will take to complete the project. Whatever the reason for the bad advice, the result is always the same – your project costs a lot more, is not finished on time, and may even require the hiring of a more professional consultant to finish the project (costing *even more* time and money).

Consider the following examples of how bad advice can adversely affect your business:

- **Paying for hardware, software, or random projects that do not reflect the scope and mission of your business.**

Let's say an incompetent IT consultant recommends you upgrade a server because they think this hardware upgrade will improve both speed and network capacity. While these things may be true, is there actually anything wrong with the hardware the consultant is recommending be replaced? How much does this new server cost? How long will it take to install and configure? And most importantly, what could this money have been spent on that might actually better reflect your business? Maybe a new Customer Relationship Management (**CRM**) solution or a data backup system? If a consultant doesn't understand what your business goals are, how can they make sound recommendations for improvement? They can't.

- **Inflated labor costs due to inexperience.**

Your incompetent consultant provides a quote for a new project. Everything seems good, and the Return on Investment (**ROI**) makes sense based on the information you are receiving from the consultant so you green light the project. The problems begin to manifest quickly because the consultant is in over his or her head. Suddenly, a project that should have taken one day has turned into a week-long endeavor, and the consultant continues to charge you for this additional time. Not only is your business affected by the downtime created by this delay, but you end up paying a lot more than the original quote. The ROI doesn't make sense anymore, but you are so far into this project that you suck it up and chalk up the lost revenue as a lesson learned. That is, of course, until it happens again.

- **Downtime, security breaches, and data loss.**

Your consultant's inexperience means that he or she often overlooks regular maintenance requirements or simply doesn't have the time and/or knowledge to spot potential problems before they occur. When a problem does occur, inexperience means that the problem takes longer to fix than it should and in some cases, can even result in catastrophic data loss. Remember the statistics from the beginning of this chapter? Now you are losing revenue because your consultant didn't fix potential issues before they became actual problems.

- **Paying to have another consultant fix a mess.**

A project isn't getting finished on time (or at all), and it becomes clear to you that it's a direct result of the consultant's incompetence. In an attempt to mitigate further costs and wasted time, you are forced to hire another consultant to finish the job. While the new consultant may fix the problem quickly, now you're stuck with invoices from two separate companies. In other words, you just paid double what you should have because you hired the wrong consultant in the first place.

- **Possible litigation costs.**

Staying with the same example about having to hire another consultant to finish the job that the first consultant was unable to complete, you are faced with either paying the guy for an incomplete job or going through the long and expensive process of litigation to retrieve compensation for lost time and money. Of course, that's assuming you can even get anything out of the incompetent consultant because they may not have insurance to cover any damages to your business or the cash on hand to reimburse you. No business owner wants to spend time in a court room, but it could happen if you hire the wrong consultant.

- **Frustration stemming from dealing with an unprofessional IT consultant.**

You will learn more about incompetent IT consultants in the next chapter, but picture for a moment the 'one-man operation'. This guy (or gal) may not have a business license, insurance, or even a storefront you can visit when attempting to track this person down to finish a job that was supposed to be finished last week. If you can't even find the person, how can you expect them to finish the work? Calling doesn't work either because it is most likely just a cell phone that the consultant may or may not answer. As a business owner, you have little to no recourse in this situation and a lot of frustration gets added to the time and money you have already wasted. Not a fun situation to be in at all.

The problem with bad advice is that it isn't always easy to put a hard dollar amount to these problems.

CHAPTER ONE

Sometimes it's easy to look at how much you've spent, but other times the soft costs of incompetence are difficult to measure. How much time have you spent tracking down your consultant? What's that worth to your business? Does frustration affect your ability to manage the business? How much revenue do you lose because you made a poor decision as a result of this frustration?

No matter how you look at it, inadequate IT support costs your business time and money that could be better spent elsewhere. As a business owner, your best line of defense against poor IT support is education. By understanding how to select a competent consultant, you can avoid all of these issues and focus on growing your business. In Chapter Two, you will learn about the various IT support options available as well as the pros and cons of each choice.

CHAPTER TWO

IT SUPPORT 101 – WHAT ARE YOUR OPTIONS?

Photo by Got Credit

Technology continues to evolve at breakneck speeds, and there are always new security threats that could endanger the integrity of your critical business data. This means that even small networks need constant maintenance from a competent computer technician to remain safe from malware, spam, latency, and data loss (just to name a few). Unfortunately, many SMBs can't afford to hire a full-time IT consultant to manage these aspects of the network, and this is where the problems begin. If you are a business owner who cannot support hiring a full-time IT consultant, you have a few options when it comes to computer and network support.

Not Doing Anything

While this seems like an obviously bad choice to most people, businesses do this all the time. Rather than being proactive, these businesses don't pay attention to the network at all until a problem occurs or something stops working. When something does go wrong, it becomes an instant emergency, and the business owner is left scrambling to find IT support immediately to figure out and fix the problem.

Waiting until something bad happens is one of the best ways to ensure network downtime, data loss, and expensive IT support. This reactive approach also results in disruptions to staff productivity, customer service, and sales.

The problem with this model is that even if everything seems to work fine, there are numerous network maintenance tasks that should be completed on a regular basis to prevent network problems. Some of these tasks include:

- Security patches
- Operating system updates
- Virus scans
- Intrusion detection
- Spam filtering
- Spyware detection
- Network optimization

If these tasks are not regularly performed, it's only a matter of time before something catastrophic happens to your business technology. This is especially true of businesses relying on specialized software products, wireless networks, and sensitive data. Regular maintenance is required to protect data from hackers and to keep everything running smoothly.

DIY Support

In an effort to save money, many business owners attempt to perform network maintenance on their own. While this option is certainly better than doing nothing at all, it's impossible for a business owner with no prior IT training to stay ahead of the technology curve while managing to effectively run their business at the same time.

In some cases, the business owner may delegate responsibility for managing the network to a tech-savvy employee. The problem with this concept is that this individual was initially hired to do a different job, and it's not feasible for this person to perform both duties efficiently. To make matters worse, the person assigned to network maintenance may know just enough to make things worse, leading to network downtime and excessive spending when experts have to be called in to fix the problem.

Some business owners try hiring a friend or relative to work as a part-time network consultant. This isn't a good idea for a couple of reasons. First, just because this friend or relative may know a few things about IT doesn't mean they are qualified to manage a business network. This could lead to problems in the long-term as this individual fails to address real network issues and only provides a temporary solution to short-term issues. Also, part-time consultants may not be available when needed because of other commitments such as work or school. If a network outage occurs during a time when this part-timer isn't available, the business suffers.

Another issue that we've seen in the past is when unqualified consultants try to take shortcuts in an effort to save money. One customer, for instance, wanted to upgrade parts of an existing network that spanned an entire warehouse as well as administrative offices. Prior to hiring professional IT support, the business owner was relying on a high school kid to perform network maintenance on a part-time basis. In effort to save the owner money, this kid installed pirated versions of Windows Server on five servers within the network. Not only is this illegal, but these bootleg versions do not receive critical security patches like a properly licensed version does. The network was at risk, and there was a host of problems directly related to the improperly licensed servers.

To correct this problem, the company was forced to spend thousands of dollars to properly license all five servers before any other work on the network could be completed. Ultimately, the project took longer and cost more than the company anticipated because network maintenance was left up to an amateur: an incompetent high school student. This decision saved the company money in the short term but cost more in the long run.

As a business owner, you also need to ask yourself; how much your time is worth? Whether you delegate network maintenance to an employee or try to keep up with it yourself, how many business-related tasks are you neglecting while spending hours trying to figure out a network issue that a professional could fix in just a few minutes? Doesn't it make sense to leave network maintenance to professionals while you focus on running your business?

Outsourcing to a Competent IT Professional

This is hands-down the best option out of the three, but even this option can often be crowded with incompetent or substandard support if you aren't careful. There are five different types of support that fall under this option and as you will learn, some of these choices are hardly better than the previously mentioned choices.

1. Vendor Support

This type of support refers to relying on phone, email or web support from hardware and software manufacturers like Dell, Microsoft, or specialized software manufacturers such as Oracle, Cisco, and Salesforce.

CHAPTER TWO

This support is usually not free, it isn't proactive and is usually very limited in scope. Not to mention that if you have ever called one of these support lines, you know how frustrating it can be. When you finally get to speak with a real person, it's usually someone based in India who is difficult to understand and has absolutely no clue about your business, your network topology, or how to address all but the most basic of problems. Vendor support is extremely frustrating and is nothing more than a waste of time and money for all but the most basic of problems, and even then it's hardly worth the trouble.

Another problem with vendor support is that these companies won't deal with anything not directly related to its product. Let's say your CRM isn't connecting to the Internet properly. You call the CRM vendor and they immediately blame to Internet Service Provider. Now you call the ISP but they determine that their service is working fine. Turns out that your firewall wasn't properly configured, but you didn't find this out for two days because you wasted time calling vendor support before finally contacting an IT professional to diagnose the problem. Had you started with this step, you could have saved two days of aggravation and prevented downtime that probably cost your business sales and revenue.

CHAPTER TWO

2. Computer Support Hotlines

While offering a slight improvement over vendor
support, these services are not suited for businesses
with mission critical IT infrastructure. Essentially,
these services charge a flat fee for 24/7 technical
support over the phone. These services may work
OK for a home user with a single computer, but
they are not capable of diagnosing the often
complex problems that can plague a business
network.

3. Part-Time IT People and New Technicians Trying to Start Out on Their Own

This type of consultant could be a technician who
was recently fired from the IT department of a
company, lost his or her job due to downsizing, or
simply left the job for some other reason. Rather
than trying to find another job, this person decides
to try starting their own IT support business
targeting SMBs.

These people aren't necessarily a bad choice. They
are usually willing to work for much less than a
professional consulting company and, in most
cases, are well-meaning. In fact, they may do an
excellent job supporting your network. That is, of
course, until they don't.

CHAPTER TWO

Keep in mind that most consultants like this are working from home. There is no office, there is no secretary, and since it's usually a one person operation, what happens when you have a mission critical IT emergency and your consultant is working on another client's network, is home sick, or is on vacation? Your business suffers because this part-time consultant is unable to rise to the challenge when you need him or her the most.

In addition to competent consultants that do not have the manpower to support your network around the clock, you also have to worry about another type of consultant in this category. This is the person who knows just enough about IT to get your business in trouble. This person may know the basics of setting up a new server, but if they don't also know how to secure that server from internal and external threats, update it properly, and create user accounts in a way that protects the integrity of mission critical business data; this consultant could be causing more harm than good. Unfortunately, due to the lack of regulation governing this industry, this scenario plays out more often than you might think and if you've ever fallen victim to something like this, you know just how tragic (and expensive) cleaning up the mess left by someone like this can be.

Guaranteeing quality work is another problem with choosing a part-time IT consultant to manage your network. These people usually do not have professional contracts that detail exactly what services you will receive, how much these services will cost, or even proper invoices for completed work. This lack of paperwork means you have little to no recourse if things go wrong. Not to mention that most of these consultants to not carry proper insurance. What happens if incompetence leads to data loss or unnecessary network downtime? There is nothing you can do except deal with the consequences of trying to save a few bucks working with an amateur. This is not the way to manage your IT infrastructure.

4. Large Tech Support Companies

On the exact opposite end of the spectrum is the massive support company with lots of technicians, many locations, and an entire support team backing up daily operations. Some of these companies are global while some may only focus on U.S.-based businesses. There are many high-quality companies that fall into this category, and all of them are capable of doing an outstanding job supporting your critical network infrastructure.

Nonetheless, there are a few problems with choosing one of these companies to support your network. First is cost. These massive support operations require a lot of capital to stay in business, and that means charging the end customer more money. For large enterprise-level companies, this isn't a problem as these businesses tend to have the budget to pay for these services. But what about the SMB? You may not have the capital to afford these services. Even if you do, you'll quickly realize the second problem with choosing one of these companies to manage your network.

As a small to mid-sized business, you represent only a fraction of the large IT support company's income compared to large enterprises that require constant attention. This means you are likely to get 'stuck' working with junior technicians that are still learning the ropes of the business. The more experienced employees are tasked with managing the networks of larger clients because they represent more profit for the company. You can't really blame the large IT company for taking this approach as it makes sense from a business standpoint, but dealing with inexperienced technicians presents many of the same problems as dealing with the part-time IT consultant already mentioned. You may not get the best advice, it could take a long time to fix an issue that a more experienced technician could fix in just a few minutes, and you are left feeling like your business doesn't really matter to the company. And when you consider the amount of money you are likely to pay for these services, it really doesn't make sense for the SMB to take this path if at all possible.

There is another issue when it comes to these large tech support companies. Your business might simply be too small for them to consider as a client. Think about local businesses that the community depends such as veterinarians, town offices, non-profits, and doctor's offices. These businesses often deal with highly sensitive personal information but may only have a handful of computers and a limited budget to spend on IT support services. Does this mean these businesses should rely on sub-standard support services simply because large IT support businesses can't be bothered? Absolutely not! Fortunately, there is another solution, and it is one that is best suited to SMBs for a variety of reasons.

5. Independently Owned IT Firms

This represents one of the best options for most small to mid-sized businesses for a few reasons. As SMBs themselves, these consulting firms are equipped to deal with the challenges of other businesses without the expensive overhead of larger IT firms. For these locally-owned companies, no business is too small, and these consultants realize that every business needs quality IT support at an affordable price.

A locally owned IT consulting business should still be large enough to provide fast response times and support at all times, but these business are still small enough to provide a more personal experience that works well with other SMB business models.

These businesses usually employ a handful of well-trained technicians that work together to solve problems for all clients. In many cases, your business will be assigned a technician who can work to solve existing problems and plan for future projects. Other technicians are also familiar with your network as well so even when your primary consultant is sick, on vacation, or otherwise unavailable, there is another equally competent technician available to answer your questions and solve issues if they arise.

Independently owned IT firms provide the professionalism you would expect from a larger IT company such as written contracts, suggested actions that reflect the scope of your business, and fast response times but typically at a lower cost and with a personal touch that you simply won't find with any of the other options discussed in this chapter.

CHAPTER TWO

While there are companies in all of the support categories mentioned previously, the independently owned consulting firm is best suited to the majority of SMBs. Even in this space, however, there are well-meaning but incompetent firms that may seem like a good choice at first glance but quickly prove otherwise through a series of unprofessional actions that make you question what you're paying for in the first place.

In the next chapter, you will learn how to choose the best IT consultant for your business based on numerous factors designed to weed out the incompetent and ill-advised consultants that are sure to do more harm than good for your business

CHAPTER THREE

EVERYTHING YOU EVER WANTED TO KNOW ABOUT CHOOSING AN IT CONSULTANT

Photo by Reyner Media

CHAPTER THREE

As a business owner, you probably don't know how to find a competent computer consultant, which is exactly why so many SMBs end up with countless horror stories about hiring the wrong consultant. Between inflated costs, excessive downtime, and unnecessary projects, there an endless number of ways an incompetent IT support consultant can literally ruin your business.

You shouldn't feel bad about not knowing how to choose the right consultant. It would be impossible for you to stay on top of all the latest technology trends while still effectively running your business. This is why you want to a hire a professional in the first place, right?

There are three primary reason why choosing the right IT consultant can be difficult. First, you don't know what you're looking for. If you don't understand the technology that makes your network function, how do you know what questions to ask of a potential computer consultant? This individual could be making recommendations for your business that seem to make sense simply because you don't know any better. Unfortunately, the consultant may not know any better either!

Second, many SMB owners believe that their business is too small to warrant the services of a professional IT support company. This idea stems from the idea that only large enterprise-level businesses require the help of a professional IT staff. Nothing could be further from the truth. No matter how small your business is, what happens when you can't send emails, when your computer gets a nasty virus, or if you lose important customer files? You do need IT support even if you only have a handful of computers – don't let anyone tell you differently.

The third reason is time. As a business owner, you are constantly dealing with something. It could be a customer issue, a problem with an employee, cash flow concerns…you get the picture. What happens is many business owners get so caught up in the daily routine of managing their business that they dismiss the idea of searching for competent IT support. These people choose to rely on the same old mediocre support that is actually hurting business productivity whether it is readily apparent or not.

While it's true that finding a competent consultant does take time, the investment in time now will save you time, money, and resources in the future. It may seem counterproductive at first, but once you have found an IT consultant that does what they say on-time and within budget consistently, you'll wonder how you dealt with incompetency for so long.

10 Characteristics of a Competent Computer Consultant

As previously mentioned, you need to make time to seek out qualified IT support unless you want to deal with the repercussions of substandard service for the foreseeable future. How do you find competent help? It starts with knowing what questions to ask of a potential consultant and looking for key characteristics that indicate you are dealing with a professional. As long as your consultant exhibits all ten of the characteristics discussed below, you can be confident that you have made a solid choice.

1. Qualifications & Experience

We've talked about this quite a bit already, but you need to understand that one of the biggest challenges about selecting the right computer consultant is avoiding the well-meaning but completely incompetent individual.

These people are not out to rip you off (at least not intentionally), but they lack the experience, knowledge, and/or tools to work on business networks. After all, even relatively simple business networks require professional attention that isn't required when setting up a home network. No matter what the shortcomings of the incompetent consultant may be, it always ends the same for the business owner: increased costs, more downtime, and a host of other adverse effects on the business that could have been avoided.

The more experienced a consultant is with working with a variety of networks, the better your chances of getting the correct repair done the first time. One mistake that many business owners make is opting to hire a junior technician that seems to have "enough" experience because they charge much less than the more experienced consultant. The problem with this strategy is that the junior consultant may take twice as long to fix the same issue meaning that your final bill is actually more expensive than if you had chosen to work with the more experienced consultant in the first place.

Junior technicians may have only seen a couple of different network configurations and if they aren't already familiar with your business's network, how can they make reliable decisions about your business technology? They can't – at least not until they learn your network and who know how long that will take. In other words, don't let your business serve as a learning environment for someone – hire someone who already knows what they are doing.

CHAPTER THREE

How to Determine a Consultant's Qualifications Before It's Too Late

It's relatively easy to sort through potential IT consultants if you know the right questions to ask. Ask the following questions to determine whether or not a particular consultant would be a good fit for your business.

1. **How long have they been in business?** If a consultant has only been in business for a year or two, stay clear. It usually takes a technician at least that long just to become proficient in the basics of network maintenance. Look for consultants with at least five years of real world experience.

2. **Has the technician worked on your type of network before?** There are so many network configurations, hardware options, and software solutions that it's impossible for even experienced technicians to have experience working with all of them. You don't want to hire a consultant with no experience working on the type of equipment your business relies on. You should ask to speak with other clients with similar networks or problems to ensure the consultant isn't just blowing smoke when

they tell you they have experience working on your type of network.

3. **Ask to see his or her resume (or that of the technicians working under them).** When you hire a new employee, you look at that person's resume and a list of qualifications before making a hiring decision. It shouldn't be any different when outsourcing IT support.

4. **Any vendor qualifications and certifications?** Consulting firms that have taken the time to become vendor-authorized are usually a good choice because the vendor has already vetted the company for you. Authorized firms are required to uphold higher standards and a level of professionalism you simply won't find in many non-certified consulting firms.

2. Client References

You'd be surprised by how many business owners skip this essential step. After all, a consultant may be a better salesperson than they are a technician meaning that they say all the right things but fail to deliver on their promises once a contract has been signed. You need to check references before making a decision about a prospective consultant. When contacting references, be sure to ask:

- Did the consultant deliver on promises?

- Was the consultant responsive when issues arose?
- Did the consultant stay on schedule and deliver on time?
- Was billing accurate and as expected?
- Would you use him or her again? Why or why not?

Also, consider asking references if there were any problems during the project. Unexpected problems happen, but the mark of a truly professional consultant is how he or she handles these problems when they arise.

3. The Importance of Multiple Technicians

It doesn't matter how skilled or experienced a technician may be, it's impossible for that individual to know everything there is to know about every type of network. Having multiple technicians at your disposal means that you benefit from the combined knowledge of multiple professionals instead of just one consultant.

Having multiple technicians available that are all familiar with your network serves another important purpose. A one-person operation can't be expected to be available at all times. Illness, vacation, and working with other clients are just a few of the reasons why relying on one person is a bad idea. If you have a network outage and your consultant isn't available, the effect on your business could be devastating.

A competent IT company uses multiple technicians that all work on projects together to some degree. This ensures that everyone is up-to-date with ongoing client projects. While you may work mostly with a single person, you know that if that person is unavailable, there are other technicians who are already familiar with your business and ready to make repairs as needed.

At Southern New England Computer Services (**SNECS**), an IT support company created by both the authors in 2002, technicians work together and discuss projects daily. Meetings are scheduled for large projects to discuss progress at the discretion of the lead tech assigned to the project. This ensures that everyone knows what's going on at any given time. Someone is always available to work on your project even when the lead technician is temporarily unavailable.

4. Availability and Response Time

When a problem arises, few things are more frustrating than waiting for support. You don't want a consultant who simply tells you to call their cell phone when something happens. What if they don't answer? How long will you have to wait for a call back or for help with your problem? You should seek to find a company that has more than one person as a backup so you can always get ahold of someone should a network issue occur.

Take the time to understand how the consultant plans to address emergency issues. A good company should be able to respond by phone within an hour and be onsite when necessary within four hours at most. This should be the same whether during regular business hours or not. For example, SNECS offers an after-hours call dispatch service. If the issue is critical, calls can be patched direct to a technician, no matter what time it is. This means that no matter what time of day or night, when a problem occurs, a solution is available quickly. Any competent consulting firm should be able to offer a similar guarantee.

5. Get Everything in Writing

When sitting down with a prospective computer consultant, that person is likely to tell you many things about how they operate their business and what kind of service you can expect if you choose to hire them to manage your network. While verbal communication is important (we'll talk about this shortly), the promises made by your consultant should all be in writing. After all, if they fail to uphold their end of the bargain and all you have is a verbal agreement, how can you actually prove what the consultant did or didn't promise as part of the deal?

You should strive to get as much as possible in writing, but there are five things that should *always* be in writing before hiring an IT consultant.

1. Payment terms – Anything and everything to do with payment needs to be in writing before a project begins. This includes the fee schedule, up-front deposit amounts, and any payments due once the project has been completed. You should also take the time to understand exactly how invoicing is done by the consultant. Many consultants, for instance, bunch all hardware, software, and labor costs together with only a lump sum at the bottom. This makes it nearly impossible to tell how much you paid for a particular piece of equipment or how many hours of labor the consultant actually charged you for the project. At SNECS, every invoice is clearly itemized by line, so you always know exactly how much you are paying for a particular product or service.

2. Compensation for missed deadlines – When a project isn't completed on time, how will the business be compensated for this delay? What about faulty work? If you experience

problems after the consultant says the project is done, what system do they have in place to make it right? Make sure all of these are clearly defined before any money exchanges hands or the project begins, or you could be stuck with substandard work and no recourse.

3. Deliverables – This should go without saying but make sure all deliverables are clearly defined in writing. What will you be able to do once the project is completed? How will these changes impact workflow? The key here is not to make any assumptions. If you expect something, make sure it is written down as part of the agreement.

4. Schedule – For your business to operate efficiently, you need to know exactly when a project will be completed. You also need to be able to plan for any scheduled downtime that occurs as a result of the project and how the project may affect the ability of your employees to perform their job duties.

5. Other guarantees – Anything else the consultant promises as part of the project should be in writing. This includes everything mentioned above as well as other promises such as how issues will be addressed, the availability of technicians if

issues arise that are somehow related to the project, and anything else that seems pertinent at the time.

6. Insurance

There are two types of insurance every qualified IT consultant should maintain for your protection. Workers' compensation insurance is the first one. This is especially important when a project requires onsite work in your office. If one of their technicians gets hurt on the job, you could be sued for medical bills and lost wages if the consulting company doesn't maintain adequate workers' compensations insurance.

Something as simple as a trip-and-fall incident could cost your business thousands of dollars if the consulting firm's insurance doesn't cover the employee for these types of injuries.

Any support company you hire should also have general business liability insurance that protects your business in the event that something goes wrong during the project. A mistake could result in excessive downtime for your business, catastrophic data loss, or equipment damage. If the company you hire doesn't have liability insurance, you could be stuck paying for these issues even though it wasn't your fault.

7. Understanding Your Business

Your network is a lot more than just a bunch of
equipment connected by cables and wires.
Information technology should be viewed as a tool
that has been specifically designed to improve
some aspect of your business. It could be increased
productivity, profits, customer relations, or
anything else that has a quantifiable positive effect
on workflow.

For this reason, your IT consultant should be
someone who is willing to take the time to
understand how your business works so he or she
can make customized recommendations that reflect
your own vision for the future of the company.
You could hire the best computer whiz in the
world, but if they are unable (or unwilling) to
understand the nature of your business, they will
not be able to make technology recommendations
that have the best interest of your company in
mind.

What you want is a business partner – someone
invested in helping your business succeed by
making sound technology recommendations. What
you don't want is a computer geek that knows the
technology like the back of his or her hand but
couldn't care less about how network changes may
affect your business. Some of the questions you

should ask yourself to determine if a consultant really has your best interests in mind include:

- Does the consultant try to understand the root cause of a problem or are they more interested in performing a "quick fix?"
- Does the consultant ask questions that demonstrate their interest in your business processes? Does he or she care about how network changes might affect your employees?
- Are the recommendations they make actually going to improve your business in some quantifiable way or are they only recommending products and services that are trendy?
- Is a training program administered by the consultant available?
- Is the consultant proactive – recommending solutions when needed – or do they wait for you to ask for assistance first?
- Does the consultant explain things in a way that you understand or do you feel like they are talking down to you by using terms that you aren't familiar with?
- Does the consultant meet with you regularly to assess how current technology is or is not meeting your business's needs?

- Does the consultant follow up with you after a project is finished to make sure you are satisfied and to answer any questions you may have?

You're paying for a consultant that cares about your business (or at least you should be). If you don't feel like your support team is actively helping you to improve your business processes by leveraging technology solutions that are relevant, it's time to look elsewhere for network support.

To illustrate this concept more clearly, SNECS always tries to think "outside the box" when clients approach us with a request. For instance, we recently had a customer mention that they would like to be able to perform inventory-related tasks faster and more efficiently.

We set up a new system using wireless scanners integrated into their existing inventory system so they could scan inventory and keep an accurate count of all in-stock items. Differences between scanned inventory counts and expected quantity based on the last report are automatically reported. We were able to streamline this tedious process using a technology solution that made sense for the customer. We try to create customized solutions for all of our clients in a similar manner – can you say that about your existing IT services company?

8. Professional Appearance and Demeanor

Although some network maintenance can be performed remotely, there are bound to be times when a network technician needs to perform work on-site in your office. Do you really want a disheveled, sloppy looking tech showing up at your place of business? It happens all too often, and if a customer sees this person walking around your office they may question doing business with you in the future.

More than that, if a consultant doesn't care about his or her appearance, it's usually a good indication that the rest of the business is just as disorganized. When hiring a consultant, make sure they are neat and clean. SNECS has a dress code that all consultants must adhere to because we understand that while our employees are in your office, we are a representative of you and your business. If your current consultant doesn't have a similar respect for your business, maybe it's time to consider a change.

9. Detailed Invoicing

As we mentioned earlier in this chapter, SNECS always provides a detailed invoice showing what each item costs. Many of our competitors only provide clients with a total so you never really know what you are paying for a particular item. You don't know if you're getting ripped off and it also makes accounting much more difficult. How do you know how much depreciation you can write off for that new server if you don't even know how much you paid for it?

When you receive an invoice from your consultant, it should specify what work was done, why it was done, and the project it is connected to at a minimum. Poor invoicing makes accounting more difficult and it could very well result in you paying more for services than you should.

10. Clear Communication

Poor communication is another concern that could result in frustration for business owners when trying to deal with computer consultants. More concerning than frustration, however, is the fact that poor communication often leads to expectations not being met, blown deadlines, and incomplete work that you are not satisfied with.

Avoiding the headaches (and expenses) associated with poor communication isn't difficult if you know what to look for. Here are some sure signs that your IT consultant is a poor communicator:

- The consultant frequently uses terms you don't understand.
- He or she frequently sticks to the basics and refrains from asking questions that would

help them to understand your business better.

- The consultant doesn't explain the reasoning behind recommendations and expects you to accept these recommendations at face value.
- Things you discuss with the consultant are not put in writing.
- He or she doesn't clearly explain how the work will be done.
- Deadlines are missed without warning or explanation.

Relationships, Attitudes, and Service

When it comes to a service provider, especially one you are developing a (hopefully) long-term relationship with, attitude is important. There are many people in the sales and service industry, and whether it be a locksmith, a baker, a mechanic or an insurance provider, there are always choices.

Why do certain people stick with a particular restaurant or always buy their cars from the same place? The reason is because that person has developed a relationship with the business. Sometimes it is a particular salesman, waitress or clerk that keeps them coming back. But what is it that started that initial connection? Maybe they happen to like the same sports team, or their kids go to school together. Sometimes, they don't have anything in common; the client just likes the personality of who is helping them.

Whatever the case is, it shows just how important a positive, friendly and upbeat attitude is to someone when they are shopping for a service provider.

A customer inquiring about service does not want to be greeted over the phone with a "WHAT DO YOU WANT?" attitude. Likewise, a current client does not want to feel like they are not important enough for your time.

A client of ours was treated like this by a previous IT company. They were told things like "Can you only call us when you have more than a few issues? We don't want to waste our time going out for just one problem." It became so bad that they were no longer asking their SERVICE PROVIDER FOR SERVICE! Imagine, paying for a service and then not using it because your service provider made you feel "bad" when you asked for help. If your service provider does not treat you with respect, it is time to find someone else.

CHAPTER FOUR

STEERING CLEAR OF DISASTER

Photo by Matt Mets

CHAPTER FOUR

This chapter is for any business owner who has experienced the expense and frustration of dealing with an incompetent consultant. When small issues that should be fixed in a matter of minutes end up taking an entire day – or worse – drag out for weeks, the negative effects on your business can add up extremely quickly.

Employees are unable to perform their job duties, customers become frustrated because they cannot conduct business with you the way they normally do, and all the while the cost of this "simple" repair continues to climb.

Another frustration that often occurs when dealing with incompetency is when a problem continues to occur even after it has been "fixed." This is when a consultant doesn't bother to understand the root cause of a problem and only slaps a Band-Aid on the problem. Within a few days, the problem is back. Aside from dealing with the same issue over and over again, the consultant will charge you for each consecutive time they come back to fix the same issue. Talk about an expensive headache!

There are countless stories of how dealing with an incompetent consultant can become an enormous hassle for you and your business. Consider this example: You hire an IT consultant to perform some network upgrades. The project is supposed to take two week in total and scheduled downtime while performing the upgrades is kept to a minimum…at least that was what you agreed to when you hired this person in the first place.

It's been nearly a month since the project started, the network upgrades still haven't been completed, and you are experiencing more network downtime than you had before the project started.

To make matters worse, now when you try to get a hold of the consultant, you are being neglected. Phone calls aren't returned promptly and when you do manage to get a hold of the consultant he or she acts like you are the problem. They agree to come back into the office the following day to look at the network but now they want to charge you *more* money to come back even though they never completed the project you originally paid them to complete.

This frustrating cycle continues until you finally can't take it anymore. You hire another consultant to fix the mess left behind by the first technician. Network downtime has already resulted in excessive customer churn, and you are left paying someone else to fix a job you already paid to have completed. This is what we call an IT horror story, and the unfortunate truth is that it happens more frequently than you might imagine. Maybe it's already happened to you. In this chapter, you will learn how to avoid these tragic circumstances and ensure your business technology projects start and finish on time, within budget, and are done right the first time. After all, you have enough on your plate dealing with the rest of your business – do you really want to spend time and money tracking down a sketchy computer consultant you left you high and dry with more network problems than you had before he or she started? Obviously not!

Not only do you, the business owner, not have time to deal with these horror stories, but the reality is that your business doesn't either. Can you afford to lose even one customer because of unnecessary network outages that could have been prevented? While some business owners may find this acceptable, we believe that most businesses cannot afford the revenue loss associated with losing a single customer in this economy.

When it comes to fixing IT-related problems, small issues should be addressed quickly and easily. Larger problems require a detailed plan and a set timeline for completion. If your computer consultant isn't providing this service for your business consistently, it's time to look elsewhere for professional computer support.

CHAPTER FOUR

Steering clear of IT disaster isn't that difficult as long as you know what causes these issues to happen in the first place and that's exactly what we're going to discuss throughout the rest of this chapter.

Determining Priorities

One of the biggest mistakes business owners make when hiring a computer consultant is failing to clearly establish priorities for a project or managed service contract. Think of these priorities as your expectations for the project in terms of speed, efficiency, price, communication, impact on workflow, and any other factors you can think of.

In other words, what's most important to you? Are you more focused on quality of work or how fast it can be done? Is price or fast response time more important to you for this project? This isn't to say that a qualified computer consultant can't provide all of these, but if there is something especially important to you or your business, make sure it is clearly communicated to the consultant before you hire him or her. And don't forget to get in all in writing too!

One way you can do this effectively is to create a list of the qualities and characteristics that are important to you (be as detailed as possible). Share this list with any consultant you are considering hiring and discuss how the consultant plans to meet these expectations throughout the project. If a consultant can't provide you with a satisfactory plan, look elsewhere for computer support.

Price

You've heard it before and have most likely experienced it too, but you definitely get what you pay for. This is especially true when it comes to service-based businesses such as IT support. That doesn't necessarily mean that paying top dollar for service is a guarantee that you will receive the absolute best service (remember our discussion about large IT support vendors in an earlier chapter?), but if your primary concern is finding a low price when shopping for a computer consultant then get ready for problems.

There's nothing wrong with trying to save a few dollars here and there, but when saving that money leads to further network problems (think lost data or unexpected network outages), that low price point won't seem so attractive anymore.

If budget is a concern, SNECS can work with you to outline major issues and projects that need to be done based on urgency and priority. This way, the issues can be resolved within your budget starting with the most critical issues. For instance, a failing server that requires replacement should be addressed before an issue with slow file transfers stemming from antiquated network equipment. Likewise, a new PC installation for an employee that hasn't even been hired yet can be delayed to stay with your business's budget. You don't have to sacrifice quality service to stay within your quarterly IT budget if you are working with a consulting firm that cares enough about your business to work through these problems with you on a priority basis. After all, Rome wasn't built in a day, right?

Testing Consultants by Starting Small

One way to get a feel for how a consultant works is to hire them for a small project such as a simple repair or a network audit before hiring them for a bigger project. This gives you an opportunity to see how the consultant performs his or her job. Did they show up on time? Complete the work as promised and within budget? Did they communicate clearly throughout the project? Do you feel comfortable working with them again?

If you feel that the consultant did a good job on the smaller project, there's a good chance they will do equally as well on larger projects too.

CHAPTER FOUR

Fixed Pricing is Always Better than an Hourly Rate

Many consultants will try to charge you an hourly rate for repairs or projects. This is beneficial for the consultant because it ensures they are paid for their time, but it could be very dangerous (and expensive) for your business. A consultant billing by the hour is likely to take much longer completing a project than one who is working for a fixed rate.

And if the consultant happens to be less than knowledgeable about a particular aspect of your network, it could take them longer to complete a relatively simple task as compared to a more experienced technician. In an hourly contract, this costs you more money.

Another benefit of demanding a fixed price is that budgeting for IT work becomes much easier and more consistent. You won't find yourself sitting at your desk with your fingers crossed hoping that a project costs less than "X" because you will know the costs well in advance of the project start date.

Get It in Writing

We've already talked about this concept in detail, but it's so important that we decided to mention it again here. The more you have in writing before a project actually starts, the less likely you are to encounter issues stemming from miscommunications and assumptions.

Some of the things you should *always* get in writing include:

- Timeline and project completion date
- Exact budget and schedule of payments
- Service guarantees (what will you be able to do once the project is finished?)
- Any expectations you have for project deliverables
- How you will receive project updates (and how frequently)
- Any responsibilities you have as the client
- Recourse if you aren't happy with the completed project

Communicating Concerns

You should never be afraid to voice any and all questions, concerns, or reservations *before* signing a contract with a consultant. You are the customer and it is the consultant's job to make you feel comfortable with a project before you begin paying for it.

Look for a consultant that is sympathetic to your concerns and one who takes the time to ease these concerns before starting a project. If the consultant is unwilling to do this or seems annoyed by your

CHAPTER FOUR

list of concerns, you are better off looking for a different IT firm to work with for this and future projects.

CHAPTER FIVE

YOU'VE FOUND THE PERFECT CONSULTANT – NOW WHAT?

Photo by The Tax Haven

CHAPTER FIVE

So you've done your due diligence and found what you believe to be the perfect computer consultant to help you with your business technology. The consultant you have chosen is competent, professional, addresses your concerns, and has a vested interested in your business, how it works, and understands how technology can improve your existing business processes.

Great!

But now what?

You want to maximize your relationship with this consultant on current and future projects because even though a good computer consultant frees you and your employees from dealing with network-related tasks, you aren't completely off the hook (and neither are your employees). There are plenty of ways you can severely jeopardize the integrity of your network even after your consultant has done everything in his or her power to correct these issues for you.

You, as the business owner, are also responsible for ensuring that the consultant knows what your business goals and priorities are at all times. After all, how can the consultant make relevant technology recommendations if they are not familiar with your vision for the future?

Only when you invest the time discussing these ideas with your consultant will he or she be able to provide relevant advice and solutions that meet your needs.

Taking Responsibility for Network Integrity and Protection

When something goes wrong with the network, many business owners immediately blame the equipment or the consultant. This can happen when a PC becomes infected with a virus, spyware, or some other issue occurs that affects the network.

Especially when it comes to viruses and other forms of malware, infection usually occurs when an end user (i.e. one of your employees) downloads a questionable file or program, disables their antivirus software, or violates security policies by using the network to access peer-to-peer file sharing (torrent) services like uTorrent and Vuze.

This highlights the importance of establishing and adhering to an Acceptable Use Policy (**AUP**). This policy governs how the network should be used and for what purposes. Your consultant can help you create one of these policies and prevent many of the issues mentioned above by regular adherence and enforcement. But we'll get back to the importance of an AUP in a minute.

Another reason why network issues can occur is failure to perform regular maintenance. This includes updates, security patches, monitoring system performance, and other preventative maintenance activities. While any competent consultant would be happy to perform these functions for your business, many business owners do not want to pay for these services that they deem 'unnecessary'. Unfortunately, failure to perform regular preventative maintenance is one of the leading causes of network failure. So, although it may not seem important when everything is working properly, you will regret the decision when something bad happens that could have been prevented.

One of the best ways to ensure all of your preventative maintenance needs are regularly met is through the use of a monthly managed service contract (like SNECS's Office Solutions Package). Managed services ensures all network maintenance is performed. We'll talk more about managed services in Chapter Six, but for now just realize that managed service contracts are the best way to prevent expensive network failures in the future.

CHAPTER FIVE

Your role as a business owner is to remain proactive in all aspects of your business, and that includes your business technology. The same goes for your employees. Take the time to train them on the AUP and the importance of network safety and security. Discuss questionable Internet activities that could compromise the integrity of the network with your employees and talk with your computer consultant about holding training sessions to reiterate these important lessons.

How Spyware, Viruses, and Other Malware Get on Your Network

Using a combination of clever techniques such as infected macros for Microsoft Office products, drive-by downloads designed to exploit popular Web browser plugins, and a variety of social engineering techniques that usually start with a spam email campaign, hackers have become extremely good at tricking end users (this includes your employees) into downloading malicious software that could destroy your network (and maybe even your business) in an instant.

Many of our clients become infected with malware by downloading programs that seem harmless. Examples include:

- Screensavers

- Emoticons
- Unconventional Web browsers or Web browser plugins
- Games
- Peer-to-peer file sharing services like uTorrent
- Music files
- Interactive banner ads
- Installing software that includes additional components that may not be readily apparent

While these are the most common ways malware is introduced to a business network, there are other ways hackers can infiltrate your technology. Many of these vulnerabilities are a direct result of failing to install the latest security patches and other preventative maintenance actions.

Many of these security vulnerabilities are referred to as zero-day exploits because when a new vulnerability is discovered and released, hackers use the published exploit to infiltrate systems that haven't yet updated to protect against this vulnerability. As a business owner, do you really have time to monitor exploits that occur all the time? In most, if not all, cases the answer is no – which is why hiring a competent computer consultant to do this preventative maintenance for you is so important.

Creating and Enforcing an AUP

An Acceptable Use Policy is a must have for any business relying on technology. This policy is a written document that states exactly what your employees can and cannot do with your business's network resources. This includes company Internet access, computers, email, and any other network component that is tied to your business in any way.

An AUP should not allow employees to download programs not approved for business use such as screensavers, pictures, music files, or file sharing networks. Essentially, the AUP should educate employees on the appropriate use of company resources.

If you don't want your employees spending time on social media sites, downloading pornographic materials, or sending inappropriate chain emails using a company email account, make sure the AUP states these things. All employees should be required to sign a document acknowledging that they have read and understood the AUP. This protects you from lawsuits stemming from sexual harassment claims and also mitigates your liability should an employee violate the AUP and cause network damage as a result.

Your computer consultant can help you create an AUP that covers most, if not all, potential threats to your network.

Being the "Dream Client" Consultants Love Working With

Many business owners feel like since they are paying for service from a vendor, whether it's a computer consultant or some other service-related field, that they have the right to be demanding and sometimes even hostile. This approach doesn't work well, especially when dealing with professional consultants.

Your relationship with your computer consultant can literally make or break your business, so maintaining a good working relationship with this person is essential to your long-term success.

The more respect and appreciation you display to your consultant, the more likely they are to "go the extra mile" for you and your business. Mutual trust and respect goes a lot further than hostility ever will. Remember, computer consultants are people too.

Three Tips for Fostering a Good Relationship with Your Consultant

1. Pay invoices on time or early.

2. Take a moment to thank your consultant for the work they have done. Let them know when you are pleased with what they have accomplished (everyone likes to know their efforts are noticed and appreciated).

3. When you have a complaint or concern, let your consultant know in a respectful manner and give them a chance to correct the issue. Also, don't forget that not all network problems are the consultant's fault so be sure to keep this in mind before jumping to conclusions about the quality of service you have received.

Basically, this all goes back to clear communication. If you are able to speak clearly and honestly with your consultant (and them with you), fostering a professional working relationship shouldn't be difficult at all.

CHAPTER SIX

THE IMPORTANCE OF PROACTIVE MAINTENANCE

Photo by J. Tools

In the last chapter, we discussed the importance of proactive network maintenance and the potentially devastating consequences that can occur when this essential task is neglected or overlooked completely. We also mentioned that we would talk more about managed services and how this is the single best way to manage the preventive maintenance requirements of your mission-critical technology resources.

How Managed Services Work and Why It's Important for Your Business

Remote management technology allows your computer consultant to perform most maintenance tasks without actually coming to the office. In fact, when done correctly, you'll never even know most maintenance is being performed, and it will have little to no impact on your business's workflow. When restarts and other disruptive maintenance actions are required, your consultant can schedule these for hours when your business isn't open (in most cases). This is the beauty of managed services.

Basically, managed services works by charging a fixed monthly fee for regularly scheduled maintenance, virus protection updates, data back-ups, security patches, network performance monitoring, and ensuring firewalls and other security settings are actively protecting your network.

Rather than hiring a full-time IT professional, managed services takes over required network maintenance for a fraction of the cost.

Benefits of Managed Services

Did you know that service calls to computer consultants for networks not under a managed service contract can take three times as long to diagnose? That immediately increases the costs of any repairs required – not to mention that the repairs might have been avoidable in the first place had the network been properly managed.

A well-managed services plan (such as the Office Solutions Package offered by SNECS) provides your business with the following benefits:

- Reduces (if not eliminates) expensive repairs and data recovery costs by detecting problems before they become network disasters.
- Faster support without higher costs. Your consultant can diagnose and repair many issues using the remote management software, saving both time and money.

- Better performance, fewer issues, and less downtime as a result of regular preventative maintenance.
- High-quality network support for a fraction of the cost of hiring even one in-house IT technician (let alone a whole team of them).
- Discounts on new projects. Most managed service clients receive discounts on custom projects and since the consultant is already familiar with your network, you will receive better, faster service compared to hiring a consultant who needs to familiarize themselves with your network before providing any recommendations.
- The fixed monthly cost of managed services makes budgeting for IT much easier than paying exorbitant amounts of money for reactive service.
- Improved data integrity. Could your business survive if you lost your mission-critical business data? Managed services greatly reduce the chances of losing critical data due to hardware or software failure.
- Can you put a price on peace of mind? Managed services free you up to manage the rest of your business without worrying about the integrity of your network.

Things to Look for in a Managed Services Plan

When shopping for a managed services plan, there is a lot of variation between what different consultants offer. That said, there are a few things your managed services plan should absolutely include:

- Security patches and updates
- 24/7 monitoring
- Spam filtering
- Virus removal and antivirus definition updates
- Vendor support
- Creation of AUP and associated training
- Hardware/software removal and installation
- User management
- Help desk support
- Working ticketing system

The Benefits of a Working Ticketing System

Having a working ticketing system is also a vital feature for any IT service provider. It provides an easy and clear way for the client to request service, inquire about new/ongoing projects, request quotes, and similar actions to their managed service provider. This creates a central place for all client requests and based on the request, the IT company can direct the request to the proper department. It also provides an easy way to audit the client's account on tickets submitted, quotes, status updates and outcomes for each request.

This way, if there was ever an issue or discrepancy about a job, both the client and the service provider can backtrack on any work requested and/or performed, review it and work towards a solution. Also, based on the ticket, it can be handled based on the urgency of the problem.

Many clients find it's better to create a ticket for something like "Setup a new email account" or "Workstation 1 is running slow, can you check it after I leave at 2pm?" It is faster and more efficient this way rather than calling in, requesting to be transferred to your account manager and explaining the problem over the phone. If the person you are looking for is unavailable, then you need to leave a message or be redirected to another person in the department.

In the time it takes to make a phone call, you could have submitted a ticket in a fraction of the time. Rather than send direct requests to one person, the entire team can work on tickets as they come in. If a tech needs to leave for a job, all the notes and correspondence is available for the next tech to pick up where the last one left off. Now, the client is waiting less time for service, and the tech is quickly up to speed on the issue at hand.

If your consultant doesn't offer these services as part of their managed services offering at a minimum, look elsewhere for a more comprehensive managed services partner. By the way, SNECS's Office Solutions Package offers all of these services for one flat monthly rate.

CHAPTER SEVEN

PRICING, CONTRACTS, AND NEGOTIATING RATES

Photo by Schlendrian.

You've probably realized by now that finding a good computer consultant takes a lot of work; but that extra effort pays for itself many times over when you avoid the potentially costly problems that stem from poor (or nonexistent) network maintenance.

That said, you don't want to throw all that time and energy away. Make sure you secure a clear contract for all services. When done correctly, there is no reason why this contract shouldn't be a win-win for both you and the consultant you have selected. A solid contract protects you from disappointment and unexpected expenses while ensuring that both you and the consultant are on the same page in terms of what is expected, how work will be completed, to what standards, and for how much money. While we always recommend having an attorney look over any contract before signing, this chapter was written to overview some of the basic things any contract for IT support should include.

Establishing Guarantees (In Writing)

Whenever you enter into a contractual agreement with a consultant, you should make sure that the contract spells out exactly what the consultant does and does not guarantee. It should be as specific as possible. For example, if you purchase a new PC through the consultant and the hard drive fails, are you responsible for making a warranty claim or does that duty fall on the consultant?

If you are unhappy with work performed, what recourse do you have? Does the consultant guarantee that the job will be revised to meet your expectations? Will they charge extra for this?

Don't be scared of a large contract that makes all these things crystal clear. Do, however, be wary of a contract that you don't understand or one that leaves many questions unanswered. The more detailed a contract is, the better protected you are from poor service.

Payment Terms

Most consultants will require a down payment before beginning any work on a project. While there is nothing wrong with this practice, do your best to protect yourself by keeping the initial payment to a minimum. Never pay a consultant in full for a project until it is finished to your complete satisfaction.

Make sure that all payments and milestones are clearly indicated in the contract and never sign a check over to the consultant unless these payment terms are defined first.

Timelines and Scheduling

This is especially important when your project is time-sensitive, and language indicating this as a priority should be included in the contract. The contract should also include terms indicating what happens if the project timeline is breached. This may include compensation for every day or week over the agreed upon completion date.

For lengthy projects, the contract should clearly define milestones that include the release of a portion of the payment to the consultant. This helps keep the consultant "on track" and makes it easier for you to follow the project's progress in relation to the agreed upon completion date.

Changes and Scope Creep

Scope creep is relatively common, especially with larger projects. Creep refers to changes or modifications that occur after the contract has been signed. Often, these change requests come from you, the business owner, as you think of additional functionality you would like your network to have.

For example, let's suppose you have decided to make some network upgrades. You meet with your consultant, agree on a cost and timeline, sign a contract, and the project begins. About halfway through the project, you realize that you would like to include Virtual Private Network (**VPN**) access for Bring Your Own Device (**BYOD**) employees who are traveling as part of their job duties. Since this was not discussed or included in the contract and it requires extra labor, software, and possibly hardware to become a reality, how does this add-on get handled?

The best way to handle this is to include language in the contract that specifies an hourly rate that the consultant will charge for changes not discussed as part of the original project. This protects you from getting ripped off if you decide to make changes to the project before completion.

Hardware and Software Costs

Most computer consultants have working relationships with a handful of hardware and software vendors. Sometimes, consultants even get discounts on these products that are not available to the general public. While the consultant probably doesn't make a lot of money on these sales, any discount you can get on these products decreases the total project cost for you.

In addition to considering the costs of equipment and software products, the contract should clearly state who is responsible for warranty claims on any equipment purchased as part of the project. Many consultants will handle this for you, but some won't. Make sure you understand what responsibilities your business has (if any) when it comes to warranty repairs on equipment.

Arbitration

Our hope is that by following the advice in this book you successfully found a competent IT consultant that will meet, and hopefully exceed, your expectations on current and future projects. Unfortunately, despite your due diligence, problems sometimes occur and it is your duty as the business owner to ensure that you are protected should this happen.

Any contract with a consultant should include an arbitration clause. Arbitration is often easier and much less expensive for both parties than wasting time (and money) in a courtroom. Just make sure both you and the consultant agree on the arbitration company before signing.

Part II

Part II

CYBERSECURITY 101

Photo by Perspecsys

INTRODUCTION TO PART II

If you recall from Chapter Five in Part I, we tried to impress upon you, the SMB owner, the importance of proactive maintenance. The idea is to find a qualified and competent computer consultant capable of performing most of these tasks for you, but as a business owner, you need to take an active role in protecting your technology assets too. This starts with creating a solid Acceptable Use Policy (**AUP**) to ensure your employees aren't endangering your network (whether accidentally or intentionally) and it's an ongoing process that includes understanding the many threats that could affect your network every day.

Part II of this book was written to provide you with the basic knowledge you need to not only speak intelligently with your computer consultant, but to equip you with enough knowledge so that you can take a more proactive role in protecting your network even when the computer consultant isn't around.

CHAPTER EIGHT

POLICY DEVELOPMENT AND MANAGEMENT

Photo by Chris Potter

CHAPTER EIGHT

As a business owner, it is imperative that you take steps to secure your network from outside threats and from inappropriate behavior by your own employees that could endanger the integrity of mission-critical business systems and data. One of the first steps to accomplishing this is the establishment of clear and robust policies created specifically to safeguard your network from these threats.

When it comes to your business's network, this is accomplished by creating a detailed AUP that should be signed by every employee with access to network resources (both local and remote). We talked about this in Part I and we will it again in a moment, but first we need to discuss another important concept: establishing security roles and responsibilities.

Establishing Security Roles and Responsibilities

One of the easiest ways to prevent potentially serious cyber security incidents is to establish a policy that clearly defines the various security roles of system users. This includes identifying company data ownership (who has access to what data) and the associated responsibilities that go along with access to that data.

For example, if your business routinely handles sensitive customer data, a chief overseer should be assigned to manage this sensitive data. This individual would be ultimately responsible for ensuring the integrity of this data including maintaining proper backups, monitoring usage, and ensuring data is protected using appropriate encryption standards. Clearly identifying who is responsible for the data within your network is a good way to foster ownership of said data and ensures that someone is always accountable for this integral part of your business.

Creating an AUP

Many businesses allow employees to use company Internet and other network resources for personal reasons throughout the day. In fact, allowing employees short breaks to check email or social media accounts helps break up the monotony of the work day and can increase employee productivity when personal usage is kept to a reasonable level.

That said, there needs to be clearly defined rules that govern the use of network resources for both personal and professional uses. This ensures the integrity of the network and significantly reduces the business's liability.

A good AUP will clearly define what types of activities are allowed while using company resources and perhaps more importantly, what activities are prohibited. For instance, downloading unapproved programs should be prohibited because of the risk of malware. Likewise, peer-to-peer file sharing software like uTorrent are known to be full of malware (not to mention they use a large amount of bandwidth and have been associated with copyright infringement). These sites should not be allowed on company network resources for this reason.

The more clearly defined your company AUP, the better. Your computer consultant can help you create a functional AUP and may even offer to train your employees in adherence. You can also find Internet resources that will assist you in making your own AUP. One such resource can be found at:

www.ITFreeFall.com/AUP

Don't Forget about Social Media

Although it's perfectly acceptable to include social media policies within the standard AUP, some business owners opt to create a separate policy for social media activities. This policy should go beyond the personal use of social media accounts by employees while using company resources – it should also include clearly defined policies for the business's social media accounts.

For example, this policy should include detailed information about when certain types of company activities should be disclosed via social media and what details can be discussed in public Web forums.

The policy should also indicate who is responsible for approving any company-related social media posts and strong password requirements whenever a new social media account is created on behalf of the company.

CHAPTER NINE

SCAMS & FRAUD

Photo by Dennis Skley

The power of technology affords your business many new opportunities that weren't available just a few years ago. Unfortunately, this technology has also cleared the way for countless online scams and fraud. Cybercriminals steal billions of dollars every year from small and mid-sized businesses. In addition to financial losses that can result from a security breach, you also need to worry about your business's reputation and the safety of your customer's information.

In this chapter, we will discuss some of the common cyber security threats that could affect your business at any moment if you're not careful.

The Dangers of Social Engineering

Social engineering is a common technique used by hackers and cybercriminals to trick unsuspecting victims into divulging personal information and/or installing malware on their computers.

Social engineering can occur offline (usually via telephone) or online via malicious websites, chat rooms, email, and Instant Messaging services. By making the interaction with your employees seem legitimate, hackers are often able to gain access to network resources by tricking employees into providing sensitive information including network access passwords or by having those employees install programs that actually contain malware designed to infiltrate the network.

Online Fraud

Online fraud takes many forms, and it isn't always clear that fraudulent activity is taking place until it's too late. Fraud may target your business and employees directly, or it may target your customers.

You can protect yourself from this threat by making sure never to divulge sensitive information such as passwords or account details via email, social media, instant messaging, or other online services. Also, let your customers know that your business will never request this information from them via these channels and any attempt to do so is most likely fraudulent. Urge customers to contact your business directly if they have any doubt about the legitimacy of a request supposedly originating from your business before providing *any* information.

Phishing Scams

Phishing is a technique used by cybercriminals to trick people into thinking they are dealing directly with a reputable business or website. As a business owner, you have to worry about this threat from two angles. First, hackers may try to impersonate your business to customers in an attempt to extract customer personal information. Second, hackers may target your employees directly by trying to steal passwords and other information that would allow them to access the network.

As a business owner, you should make sure that your customers understand that your business will never ask for personal information via email. Any official communications sent from your business should also include a disclaimer in the signature line that reminds customers of the fact that the business will never ask for personal information.

Your computer consultant should also be able to assist with training employees on the dangers of phishing scams. Employee awareness is the best defense you have against phishing scams so the more time you spend educating your employees about how to handle these threats, the more secure your network becomes.

Rogue Antivirus Offers

Fake antivirus is an extremely popular tactic for hackers. These rogue programs are nothing more than a virus that tries to extort users of the infected machine into purchasing a product that may or may not solve the problem.

Accidental virus infections are unavoidable. Your employees need to understand what to do when an infection occurs. Usually, this involves notifying your IT consultant immediately of the issue so damage to the network can be mitigated.

Other Malware Threats

If the malware examples above seem frightening, just know that those threats only represent the tip of the proverbial iceberg. Keylogging software can be packaged in with just about any software download and allows hackers to record every key pressed by your employees.

Many hackers have recently started resorting to an old technique that is still effective – creating rogue Word documents with malicious macros embedded within the file that install malware as soon as the file is opened. This threat is almost exclusively spread through email. Again, educating your employees about these threats is the best protection you can provide for your network and mission-critical business data.

There are thousands of malware threats trying to infiltrate your network every day. This is another reason why hiring a competent IT consultant is so important. This individual or team can guide you through the proper steps you and your employees must take to protect your network from an endless malware assault.

CHAPTER TEN

NETWORK SECURITY

Photo by Yuri Samoilov

When it comes to securing your company's network, there are three things you need to consider:

1. Identifying all devices and network connections
2. Setting boundaries between your network, the Internet, and other networks
3. Enforcing controls and policies that prevent misuse, unauthorized access, and denial of service (**DoS**) events

This chapter is devoted to looking at these considerations in detail, so you understand the basics of protecting your network from outside threats.

Securing the Internal Network and Cloud Services

Your business network needs to be insulated from the public Internet using a combination of strong user authentication (good passwords) and policy enforcement equipment including firewalls and Web filtering proxy servers. Antivirus software and intrusion detection systems should also be used to identify unauthorized attempts to access the network. You don't necessarily need to know how these work to protect the network as long as you know they are necessary. Your computer consultant should be more than happy to explain these concepts in more detail if you are so inclined.

Cloud services are those services which are hosted off-site by another provider but could contain mission-critical data or functionality. Office 365, a Microsoft cloud-based Office suite, is an example of a cloud service. Although you have limited control over how these cloud-based services protect your data, you should spend a few minutes reviewing the terms of service to ensure your information is safe with these providers. You can also ask your consultant to review these documents as well.

Enforcing Strong Password Policies

The best way to secure your network from weak passwords is to employ two-factor authentication. This requires a user to provide two different types of evidence that they are who they say they are. One of these is usually a static password; the other could be a personal security token that constantly displays changing passcodes. Although two-factor authentication is the best, it is not always practical.

It is for this reason that you should have a strict password policy in place that encourages employees to create passwords that aren't easy to crack. You'd be surprised at the number of people that use passwords such as "password" or the name of their dog as a password. These passwords are easy to guess and easy to crack using brute force hacking techniques (where a dictionary program guesses letter and number combinations until a match is found).

As a general rule, passwords should be at least 10 characters long, contain a combination of letters and numbers, and employees must be instructed not to write them down or reuse the same password for multiple accounts.

Securing Wi-Fi

Many businesses choose to offer wireless service to customers, guests, and visitors. While there is absolutely nothing wrong with this practice, these guest networks should never be connected directly to the main company network. If the traffic between the two networks crosses paths at any time, there is a risk that sensitive data from the primary network could be compromised.

Another consideration when dealing with wireless networks is the encryption protocol used to secure the network from the outside. The only encryption standard your network should use is Wi-Fi Protected Access 2 (WPA2) encryption because older standards like WEP are too easy to hack.

Encrypting Sensitive Data

In addition to adhering to regulatory requirements governing information safeguarding, all sensitive company data should be encrypted. This ensures that even if hackers are able to infiltrate the company network, the data will still be protected.

Many of the notorious security breaches that have occurred in recent months would have been much less severe had the data been properly encrypted. Never overlook the importance of safeguarding your company and customer data – always encrypt any information that could be damaging if it were to fall into the wrong hands.

Regular Application Updates

All systems, software, and networking equipment should regularly be updated as patches and firmware upgrades become available. This is especially important for wireless networking equipment because these devices don't usually notify users that firmware updates are available like Windows, and many third party applications do.

Whenever possible, using automatic updating services is the best way to ensure your hardware and software is always protected with the latest security updates.

Using VPN for Remote Access

Many companies allow employees to access internal company resources remotely. This is useful for employees working from home or those who frequently travel on company business. While there is nothing wrong with allowing employees to access these resources remotely, it must be done in a secure manner and the best way to accomplish this is to employ a Virtual Private Network (**VPN**).

Using two-factor authentication relying on either hardware or software tokens, you can ensure that the only people accessing your network remotely are your own employees. Failure to implement VPN services for remote access could allow hackers to intercept any Internet traffic coming and going from your internal network.

CHAPTER ELEVEN

WEBSITE SECURITY

This website has been hacked by
=cipher=

Photo by Salim Virji

CHAPTER ELEVEN

Just about every business needs a website to remain competitive, and this means that website security has become more important than ever. Hackers know that your company probably has a Web server and the information contained within that machine can be extremely valuable on the black market.

Cybercriminals spend a large amount of time searching for Web servers that haven't been properly secured. Not only can an improperly secured Web server leave your business data open to compromise, but it can also affect how your customers perceive your business.

Most customers agree that website security is one of the biggest considerations when they choose to shop or do business via the Internet. If your website isn't secure, customers won't use any online services your business offers – potentially resulting in loss of revenue and legal liabilities for your business.

Some of the threats to your web server that you need to consider include:

- Exploitation of software bugs in the Web server in an attempt to gain unauthorized access to files and folders that are not meant to be publicly accessible.

- Denial of Service (**DoS**) attacks that could prevent your Web server from functioning properly.
- Sensitive information could be modified without authorization.
- Unencrypted information traveling between the Web server and the client browser could be intercepted and used for a variety of nefarious purposes.
- Website defacement
- Access to other parts of your business network via a vulnerability in the Web server
- Once hacked, your Web server could be used for illegal purposes such as distribution of pornography and pirated software.

Proper Planning is Essential

Once a Web server is online, it is freely available for the public to access. This makes it especially important to ensure that all security considerations have been taken into account before a Web server goes live. While taking the time to properly plan *any* technology implementation is always recommended, never underestimate the importance of doing it right the first time when it comes to any equipment that is on the public side of your network. Failure to implement a Web server properly could result in catastrophic problems for your business.

Web Server Operating Systems

Unlike most of the machines inside your company network, many Web servers do not run on Windows – instead they run on Linux (the Apache Web server is a popular, free Web server). There is absolutely nothing wrong with this, but even a consultant who is well-versed in Windows Server may know nothing about properly configuring a Linux server for secure operation.

Many of the vulnerabilities typically exploited in Web servers are a direct result of improper configuration so make sure whoever sets up the Web server knows what he or she is doing. Some of the basics that any Web server configuration should include are:

- Patching and upgrading the Operating System (**OS**)
- Changing all default passwords
- Removing any unnecessary services or applications
- Configuring user authentication
- Installation (and configuration) of security controls and applications
- Security testing

If these actions are not performed (at a minimum) prior to taking your Web server live, you are almost guaranteed to have problems soon after going online.

Monitoring the Content Published on Your Website

The first place hackers often look for information about businesses is the company website. This information is often used in social engineering scams, i.e. the hackers find out the name and other personal information of the Chief Executive Officer (**CEO**) and they attempt to impersonate that individual to other employees or customers in an attempt to gain access to company resources. This is only one example, however. There are countless other ways the information on your company website can be used by cybercriminals for illegal activity.

It is for this reason that it becomes so important to establish a Web publishing process and policy that clearly explains what information should be published for public viewing, who is responsible for approving content for Web publishing, and how changes to content already published on the Web should be handled.

As a general rule, there are certain things that should not be published on a Web server including:

- Proprietary business information
- Information that pertains to your company's security
- Medical records (both employee and client)
- Physical and information security safeguards and protocols
- Details about your business' network infrastructure, current IT projects, or other sensitive network information including IP addresses and access codes

Preventing Unauthorized Access

The purpose of your Web server is to make content available to the public, but the very fact that this information is publically accessible means that its integrity is questionable compared to data stored on the internal network.

To ensure the safety and integrity of all data on the network (both public and private), specific resource control practices should be put in place, including:

- Only install necessary services

- Web content should be installed on a dedicated hard drive (physically separated from other content)
- All scripts and external programs executed as part of Web content should be stored in a single directory
- Disable hard links
- Disable directory listings
- Use robust user authentication
- Employ intrusion detection systems and file integrity checks
- Protect backend servers (such as databases) from command injection attacks

Beware of Active Content

Active content, such as that created using JavaScript or Flash, makes your website dynamic and allows for a level of interactivity with the end user that isn't possible when using only static Web content.

Unfortunately, active content is one of the easiest ways for hackers to access your Web server and possibly even your internal network. Although we don't recommend getting rid of all active content on your website, you should only use it when necessary to improve the user experience. Be sure to incorporate all security patches for active content as soon as it is released to mitigate the risk of zero-day attacks affecting your network.

One final note about active content – many businesses rely on a popular open source content management system (**CMS**) called WordPress to run the front and backend services of the company website. WordPress is inherently secure and is fully customizable using plugins that are created by third-party developers. Unfortunately, these plugins offer hackers a way into the website when they are not properly updated. To make matters worse, some of these plugins can be rather expensive, and many webmasters will look for a bootleg, or pirated, versions of the plugins to circumvent these costs.

A recent wave of cyberattacks targeting WordPress-powered websites revealed that many of these pirated plugins were loaded with malware that allowed hackers to gain remote administrative privileges to the WordPress backend. Ensure that any plugins or active content used on your business's website are legitimate and fully backed by the developer as being malware free and regularly updated.

CHAPTER TWELVE

EMAIL

Photo by Yoel Ben-Avraham

Email is a critical part of every business. Most communications within the company and when communicating with customers is conducted using email and, as a result, email has become another favorite target for cybercriminals.

Spam Filtering

Did you know that nearly 60% of all email received by your business is either spam, a phishing attempt or otherwise unsolicited email? Email has also become one of the easiest ways for hackers to spread viruses and other malware.

Protecting against spam email is relatively easy. By combining an email filtering service (usually available from your email provider) with a locally installed email filter, you should be able to eliminate most of the spam email your employees deal with every day. This greatly reduces the chances that your network will become infected with malware as a result of a phishing scam or an email with malware embedded within an attachment.

Employee Training

Even with proper spam filtering in place, some rogue emails are bound to slip through the cracks and end up in the inboxes of your employees. When this happens, your employees become the last line of defense against a possible network catastrophe.

Training your employees in security awareness, the dangers of spam and phishing campaigns, and the appropriate use of company email services is an important aspect of mitigating this threat. Employees should also be instructed on the procedure to follow if they receive an email they deem to be suspicious.

Employee training can be made more effective by following up on a regular basis. This can be done by sending out a security awareness newsletter every month, sending out urgent bulletins about known phishing scams in the headlines, and bi-annual refresher courses on general email and network security best practices. By keeping the constant threats presented by email in the front of your employees' minds, they are more likely to remember what to do when something suspicious lands in their inbox.

Sensitive Information and Email Don't Mix Well

By its very nature, email is not intended to be a secure transmission medium. It mostly relies on plain text protocols that are easily hacked or "spoofed". Spoofed is when a hacker sends an email from one email address but makes it look like it came from another (usually trusted) email address. On top of that, it's extraordinarily easy to send information to the wrong email address. At the very least, this results in embarrassment for your business; at worst, it could become a lawsuit and damage your business's reputation beyond repair.

To counteract these potential issues, your business should have a policy that clearly indicates what information can and cannot be shared via email. Employees should be trained to understand the dangers associated with including too much personal information via email, and the customer should understand that your business will never ask for personal or sensitive information via email. This protects your business and your customers.

Email Retention Policies

Many of us are guilty of letting our personal email accounts become ridiculously full. Sometimes it's because we simply don't take the time to dispose of old emails and other times it's more akin to a packrat mentality (we never know when we might *need* a particular email). While this issue is negligible when it comes to personal email accounts, you shouldn't be so lax with business email accounts.

Between the costs of storage and backup and the legal and regulatory requirements that may be imposed, it makes sense to keep email inboxes under control. An email retention policy is the best way to do this. Many businesses use a 60 or 90-day retention policy so email doesn't get out of control. Obviously, there will always be exceptions to this rule such as emails that have a quantifiable importance to daily operations, but these emails should be only a small portion of the overall email handled by your company's email service.

Developing an Email Usage Policy

Just as we discussed the importance of an Acceptable Use Policy for network resources, your business should have a clear email usage policy that addresses key issues such as what company email should and should not be used for as well as what data can be transmitted. Privacy, acceptable use, and retention policies should also be addressed.

In addition to protecting your business and your customer from security threats related to email usage, this policy also explains to employees what they can do with company resources. We've all seen chain emails (some cute and some downright inappropriate for the workplace) – a clearly written email usage policy can prevent these types of emails from being sent across your network while holding those who violate the usage policy accountable for their actions.

You can find a sample email usage policy at:

www.ITFreeFall.com/Email

CHAPTER THIRTEEN

MOBILE DEVICES

Photo by Tribehut

CHAPTER THIRTEEN

In the last few years, we have seen the use of mobile devices explode in the workplace. Cell phones, tablets, e-readers, and personal laptops access company resources from within and outside the network all the time. Unfortunately, this can pose a serious security risk to your technology assets. This is especially true of companies who have adopted Bring Your Own Device (**BYOD**) policies that allow for the use of personal electronic devices to access company resources.

Many of these devices are used for personal reasons outside the office – a practice that makes these devices especially susceptible to malware infection. Once a device becomes infected, hackers have an open door into your network unless precautions are taken to mitigate these risks up front.

A recent mobile security survey conducted by Symantec reported that 68% of respondents ranked loss or theft of mobile devices as the most serious security concern and 56% stated that mobile malware was the second concern. Mobile malware has become increasingly dangerous for businesses opting to employ a BYOD program – remember that even though your employees may be responsible for their devices, your business is still responsible for the data contained on those devices.

Some of the top threats that target mobile devices in the workplace include:

- Data loss or compromise
- Social engineering
- Malware
- Threats to data integrity
- Web and network-based attacks

Despite these concerns, you can protect your company resources from the threats imposed by mobile device use by following a few simple steps that ensure your technology resources and data assets are protected.

Security Software

Most of the major antivirus and Internet security companies offer mobile device products in addition to their PC and Mac product lines. By enforcing a policy that any mobile device connected to your business network have one of these security programs installed, you can limit hackers' ability to steal information from the device or from your business.

Ensure Software is Up-to-date

Just like the computers within your business network, mobile device operating systems (Android, iOS, and Windows) require regular updates to remain protected from security threats.

Always make sure these devices are equipped with the latest updates to the OS and any third party applications.

Encryption

All modern mobile operating systems contain the technology to encrypt all data stored on the device. In the event that the device is lost or stolen, thieves will not be able to access the encrypted data. This protects any personal information on the device but, more importantly, it protects your business data from being compromised.

Password Protection

In addition to encrypting sensitive data stored on the device, employees using mobile devices on your company network should be required to use a strong device password. If the device is stolen, this acts as an extra layer of protection to keep any data contained on the device safe from prying eyes.

Reporting Procedures for Lost/Stolen Equipment

If a device used on the company's network is ever lost or stolen, every employee should be instructed on the proper reporting procedures so your computer consultant can take the necessary steps to mitigate any further losses and threats to the network.

You should also have a procedure in place to deactivate the device and wipe all data remotely. Many of the mobile security software suites designed for mobile devices offer this functionality as part of a premium service. If a device is lost or stolen, this additional functionality is well worth the small fee associated with the subscription.

Disposal Procedures

Just as there should be a documented process for reporting and handling lost or stolen equipment, there should be a similar policy for handling old equipment that is deemed "End of Life." These devices may still contain sensitive information and even though these devices may be deactivated, this data may still be accessible should the discarded device fall into the wrong hands.

As a side note, SNECS provides full protection and monitoring of all mobile devices connected to your network as an add-on to our Office Solutions Plans.

CHAPTER FOURTEEN

EMPLOYEES

Photo by Colin

Employees are the single biggest threat to your network security, although usually it's not intentional; hence the importance of establishing clear policies such as an AUP that details appropriate use of company resources. These policies help prevent honest employees from making mistakes that could endanger mission-critical business data and resources.

Another issue that all business owners must face is those dishonest employees who may choose to endanger your business assets intentionally. This could be a result of these employees simply not caring to follow established AUPs, but it could also be the result of an employee intentionally trying to cause harm to your network or access sensitive data for nefarious purposes.

Failure to exercise due diligence when hiring employees could result in a legal and financial nightmare for your business. Harassment, violence, embezzlement, and lawsuits for negligent hiring could all become a reality if you don't take the time to screen potential new hires before making the job offer.

Vetting Job Candidates

Depending on the size of your organization, the hiring process could be very complex or extremely simplified. While neither is right or wrong per se, it is imperative that you properly vet any potential candidate for employment before making a job offer. Whether candidates are required to go through a series of interviews with various levels of management or you sit down with a prospective employee for a one-on-one before making a hiring decision, there are certain steps you simply shouldn't skip when hiring new people.

We don't want to tell you how to run your business, but we do want to make sure your network and mission-critical technology assets are protected from people who may want to exploit your business. The fact that you're reading this book means that you want to protect your network assets as well – which is why properly vetting employees is so important.

To learn more about how to properly screen employees prior to hiring, there is an online employment screening resource called the "Online Safe Hiring Certification Course." This course teaches what to look for in a potential employee during various stages of the hiring process and is an excellent way to improve your current hiring practices. The course can be found at:

<u>www.ITFreeFall.com/Hiring</u>

In addition to properly screening employees throughout the hiring process, performing background checks and verifying education and other credentials should be a priority. With so many people falsely representing themselves when applying for jobs, it only makes sense to make sure that people really are who they say they are before putting them on the payroll.

Some of the things you should check before hiring any employee includes:

- Verification of prior employment
- Verification of education credentials
- Criminal background checks
- Drug testing
- Sex offender registries
- Social security validation

In some cases, it can get expensive to verify all this information. This is why properly vetting candidates first helps to narrow down the playing field before you start looking into verifying this information. Also, keep in mind that if your business does perform background checks on prospective or current employees, you are bound by the Fair Credit Reporting Act (**FCRA**). Ensure you are in compliance with the FCRA. You can find out more about your obligations as an employer under this legislation at:

www.ITFreeFall.com/Know

Setting Appropriate Access Controls

Internal company data, as well as customer information, is confidential and should only be viewed when there is an actual need. As a business owner, it is your responsibility to evaluate the roles and responsibilities of every employee to make sure they have access to everything they need to perform their job functions properly *without* providing them access to information they do not need.

If your business does not currently have a system or policy in place for controlling data access, consider the following precautions as recommended best practices. Employees should:

- Not access client information without a valid reason.
- Never provide confidential data to anyone without being absolutely sure of the identity and authority of that person.
- Not use client data for testing, development, training, or any other purpose that doesn't serve the client's needs or some other necessary business function.
- Always use secure transmissions techniques when transferring sensitive information.
- Only keep confidential data for as long as it is deemed necessary.

- Keep work areas clean and free from confidential information that could be viewable by other employees or customers.
- Properly dispose of all printed documents using approved procedures (document shredding services, shredding within the office). Likewise, electronic data should be disposed of using approved methods that ensure the data is really gone once removed from the machine (electronic shredding functionality comes with many software security suites).

Proper Security Training for Employees

Just as it's important to properly train your employees in network usage, security awareness training is one of the best investments you can make for the security of your network. The more employees understand about system vulnerabilities and threats to the network, the better prepared they will be when faced with a questionable situation that could result in a compromised network if not handled correctly.

Creating a robust IT security program means incorporating training on security policies, procedures, and techniques. It should also include training in management and operational controls designed to keep IT resources safe.

Never underestimate the importance of properly training your employees in these areas of your business. Technology users in your business are the single most important group of people when it comes to reducing network vulnerabilities.

CHAPTER FIFTEEN

PHYSICAL SECURITY

Photo by David Goehring

CHAPTER FIFTEEN

There are numerous threats that can affect your company network remotely such as malware, social engineering, and phishing scams. These threats are a constant concern for the SMB and should not be overlooked. That said, there is another threat that many business owners forget to think about: the physical security of your business.

What many people do not realize is this: if a cybercriminal gains physical access to your equipment, there is little that even the best intrusion detection system or security software can do to stop that individual from creating absolute havoc. From stealing confidential information to destroying mission-critical files, the possibilities are nearly endless when physical security isn't taken seriously.

The Importance of Securing Your Facility

Physical security comes in many forms. Sure…gates, locks, and access control are all important aspects of this concept, but there are less obvious physical security threats that many people overlook. One of these threats is maintaining the security of public spaces. For example:

- Employees should be instructed to orient their computer monitors in such a way that they are not viewable from public spaces.

While all employees should follow this rule, it is especially important for employees who routinely deal with sensitive information.

- Employees should never write down login or password information where they can be seen by others (employees or customers). Think about how many times you've seen sticky notes affixed to the edge of a computer monitor – it is a serious security risk, and hackers look for these types of security blunders all the time.

- Any equipment that is easy to remove (such as mobile devices) shouldn't be left in areas where a customer could grab the device without being noticed.

Be Mindful of Printed Materials Containing Sensitive Information

Hackers, cybercriminals, and identity thieves love printed documentation that isn't disposed of properly. It's amazing how much information can be obtained from a person or a business simply by going through the trash at the end of the day. The best way to prevent this from happening is to limit the amount of sensitive information that is printed in the first place.

Employees should be instructed in any policies that govern what kind of information can be printed in the first place as well as procedures for properly disposing of any printed materials that does contain sensitive information. Usually, a document shredding service is the best way to ensure criminals don't get access to these files. If your budget doesn't allow for hiring such a service, instruct all employees to shred documents as soon as they are no longer needed. Becoming lax with printed materials is a surefire way to invite unauthorized access to potentially mission-critical data.

Securing Snail Mail

Even though we rely on technology for many of our daily tasks, some things are still done the old-fashioned way. Mail is one example. Many of the bills your business receives probably still comes in via regular mail. If you're not careful, these items could end up in the hands of hackers looking for information they can use to start a social engineering attack on your business.

Make sure mail is picked up promptly, and any outgoing mail is handled in a manner that ensures its safety until picked up by the mail carrier. In other words, don't leave mail sitting in a publicly accessible mailbox overnight as it could quickly find its way into the wrong hands.

CHAPTER SIXTEEN

OPSEC

Photo by Got Credit

Operational security (**OPSEC**) is a term originally devised by the military, but we can apply many of these principles to securing your business as well. In this context, OPSEC refers to preventing hackers from gaining access to information that could ultimately lead to a network breach. It's about identifying areas that could present a security risk and then creating solutions that help protect your mission-critical data and assets from these threats.

There are five distinct actions that make up the OPSEC process. Keep in mind that OPSEC isn't a one-and-done type of thing – it is a continual process that needs to be regularly revisited to ensure successful implementation of its principles.

The five components of OPSEC are:

- Identify mission-critical information
- Analyze any threats to that information
- Analyze business vulnerabilities that could allow a hacker to access said information
- Assess the risks to your business if this information was obtained by hackers
- Apply countermeasures to mitigate these risk factors

Identifying Critical Information

The first step in OPSEC is identifying the critical information that is both critical to your business and potentially dangerous in the hands of cybercriminals. Some of this information includes:

- Customer information
- Contracts
- Patents and other intellectual property
- Leases/deeds
- Policies and other documentation related to internal business functions
- Corporate paperwork
- Audio tapes
- Video tapes
- Strategic planning meeting minutes

This is just a generalized list. There may be many other forms of mission-critical data depending on the type of business you own and how much of this business relies directly on technology.

Analyzing Threats

Once you have determined what information is critical to your business, you need to figure out what potential threats to this information exist. You can do this by asking yourself a series of questions designed to establish likely threats.

- What cybercriminals would be interested in this information? (Competitors, hackers motivated by politics, etc.)
- What are these hackers' goals?
- What would these hackers likely do with the information if obtained?
- What publicly available information might these cybercriminals already have access to that could assist them when infiltrating your network?

Analyzing Vulnerabilities

This action is meant to identify the vulnerabilities within your current business model as it pertains to protecting mission-critical data. During this part of OPSEC, you need to take a good look at everything your employees do on a daily basis, what policies (if any) you have in place to protect the network, and finally, compare your findings with the threats identified in the previous step. Common vulnerabilities for SMBs include:

- Mobile devices that aren't secured properly (refer to Chapter Fourteen)
- Inadequate or nonexistent policies about data protection
- Storing of critical information on personal email accounts or other non-company networks

- Lack of policy related to using social media for business purposes

Assessing Risk

To properly assess risk, you must consider two components. First, the vulnerabilities identified in the previous step must be analyzed so possible OPSEC measures can be established to mitigate these threats. Second, the costs of time, resources, and personnel must be assessed when considering ways to mitigate these threats.

If the cost to achieve protection exceeds the costs associated with exploitation of one of these vulnerabilities, then it doesn't make sense for you to take action on that particular OPSEC measure. This process must be followed for every vulnerability identified during the third action and every decision pertaining to OPSEC risk assessment should be approved by you or a designated appointee in charge of implementing OPSEC for your business.

Applying OPSEC Countermeasures

Once you have determined which OPSEC measures are feasible to implement, these actions should be applied to your current business model. Be prepared for additional costs when applying these countermeasures. As long as you have established that these actions are deemed

appropriate based on the vulnerability they
prevent, these costs are justified and, in fact,
necessary for the security of your business.

CHAPTER SEVENTEEN

PAYMENT SECURITY

Photo by Sean MacEntee

CHAPTER SEVENTEEN

If your business accepts payment by debit or credit card, you are immediately at a much higher risk for exploitation by hackers. In other words, you have to take extra precautions to ensure your data is safe. In addition to ensuring the safety of any payment information you collect or store, there may be additional security requirements set forth by the bank or payment processing service. These regulations are in place to help prevent fraud and should never be dismissed as excessive or 'not necessary'.

It's important to realize just how prevalent card fraud is. Just in the last year, Target lost payment information for over 40 million customers after hackers targeted the POS systems in retail stores. This information wasn't encrypted meaning that hackers were able to use this credit card information without further effort. This data was then sold on the black market and used to make fraudulent purchases around the world.

Home Depot was affected by a similar IT security disaster when it was discovered that malware had been installed on the Self-Checkout machines in hundreds of its stores. Once again, this information wasn't encrypted, and hackers were able to make fraudulent purchases with the stolen data.

Keep in mind that these are massive corporations with enormous IT budgets, and they still fell victim to cybercriminals. It's reasonable to assume that the same thing could happen to your business – especially if you handle customer payment information on a regular basis. That is, of course, unless you take the time to establish security policies that protect this information from dangerous hackers and other cybercriminals.

Understanding the Data You Keep

The first step in protecting customer payment information is understanding exactly what data your business uses, where it is kept, and who has access to this information on a regular basis.

Start by making a list of all the customer information you collect and keep. This includes the names, addresses, payment information, Social Security numbers, and bank account details. Criminals don't only look for payment information – anything that can be used to commit identity theft is also extremely valuable on the black market.

You also need to evaluate whether or not you actually *need* to keep all the data you store on your network. You may not realize how much of your customers' data you are actually storing and you may be surprised to learn that you could probably

144

do without storing some of this data. The less information available for hackers to steal, the less of a target your business becomes to hackers.

When you determine that storing certain data is essential to business operations, look for ways to safeguard this information using security tools and services that have been recommended by the payment industry. These recommended tools have been validated against industry security requirements and provide a layer of protection above and beyond the normal network security measures you have in place for your business technology assets.

Encryption of all payment data is another essential security step your business should take to safeguard sensitive customer information. Even if hackers do access your network, modern encryption standards are strong enough that it would take a room full of supercomputers months – maybe even years – to break the encryption key.

Access Control

When it comes to payment security, there are two main components to ensuring proper access control. The first is making sure that any computers used for payment processing are not used for mundane tasks like surfing the Internet. Activities, like surfing the Web, using social media, and accessing personal email from the same computer that payments are taken from, is an invitation for disaster. Keep payment processing equipment separated at all times to avoid potential problems down the road.

The second component is controlling employee access. In other words, only allow employees who actually need to access payment information the ability to view, edit, or modify this information. Whether through malicious intent or ignorance, employees who don't need access to sensitive information are an unnecessary security threat.

CHAPTER EIGHTEEN

INCIDENT REPORTING

Photo by Tex Texin

CHAPTER EIGHTEEN

No matter how well you protect your network from intrusion, there may come a time when your business falls victim to a cyberattack. For this reason, you need to establish procedures for reporting any incident that could jeopardize the sensitive information of your customers and other mission-critical business data. Proper and timely reporting is one of the best ways to mitigate damages caused by a breach of your network – do not skip this important step.

There are three types of breaches that could occur at your business:

- *Physical breaches* – This includes theft, burglary, and other physical crimes against your business. In addition to any losses of hardware that could occur during a physical breach, you should also be concerned with the exploitation of potentially sensitive data found on these machines and any printed materials that might have contained customer data stolen during the breach.
- *Network security breaches* – These are events where computers on your network have become infected with malware, are access by cybercriminals remotely, or are used by unauthorized individuals for malicious purposes.

- ***Data breaches*** – This is when sensitive information is leaked to hackers by either of the two types of breaches mentioned previously. Data breaches can also occur when data is improperly handled (such as not shredding documents containing sensitive business or customer information).

Notify Law Enforcement (if necessary)

Depending on the type of breach that occurred, the first step in discovering a breach is to notify local law enforcement and any relevant government agencies about the breach. If customer information has been exposed, customers should be notified of the breach as soon as possible.

Work with Leadership Teams to Mitigate Damage

After a breach, business decision makers and technical leadership must work together to determine an effective containment plan. While this containment is likely to vary depending on the exact nature of the breach, but idea is always the same: prevent further damage by notifying affected parties promptly and eliminating the vulnerability responsible for the breach in the first place.

Recovery

Once a proper containment plan has been established and executed, recovery efforts should begin as soon as possible. This is also the time when any remaining traces of the breach can be eradicated. For instance, if the breach resulted in a malware infection, all instances of the rogue software should be removed, and the network access privileges of any user accounts involved in the breach should be disabled.

Some of the key disaster recovery principles that you should think about in the aftermath of a breach include:

- *Don't wait* – SMBs should never wait any longer than absolutely necessary to make changes that would have prevented a breach from occurring the first place. Obviously, there may be budgetary and resource concerns when implementing recovery strategies, but the costs of preventing another breach far outweigh the damage to your business reputation should another event occur after the first breach.
- *Protect information* – As an SMB owner, you need to implement appropriate security and backup solutions to reduce the risk of

losing essential business data following a breach.

- *Employee involvement* – While some degree of downtime following a breach is expected, your employees play a key role in reducing the amount of downtime required to properly recover from a breach.

- *Regular testing* – Anytime a change is made to your network infrastructure, be sure to test the system fully. You don't want to wait until after a breach occurs to find out that essential data wasn't properly backed up and could be lost forever.

- *Be prepared* – Although the cost required to invest properly in improvements following a breach, these costs pale in comparison to not addressing the issues that left your network vulnerable to exploitation in the first place. Assuming your business survives the first breach, there is a very small chance it will fare as well should a second breach occur due to inaction on your part.

Learning from the Incident

One of the most important aspects of recovering from a disaster is actually learning something from the mistakes that led up to the breach in the first place. One of the most effective ways to accomplish this is to hold a "lessons learned" meeting with every employee in attendance. This meeting helps to explain what went wrong, what steps were taken to correct the issue, and most importantly, what can be learned about network security as a result of the breach.

Taking the time to understand these concepts will help to prevent future breaches and provide employees with an understanding of the importance of network security – hopefully fostering a more proactive attitude about protecting network resources.

THANK YOU FOR READING

A QUICK WORD FROM THE AUTHORS

Dear Reader,

We hope you enjoyed IT Free Fall: A Business Owner's Guide to Avoid Technology Pitfalls. Technology is an amazing thing. It allows us to reach new customers, analyze mission-critical business data like never before, and increase the productivity of our employees.

Despite all the benefits of technology, many small business owners allow their IT resources to go down the drain – into an IT Free Fall. Is it because they don't care? Maybe they think they can't afford proper IT support? Perhaps they think their business is too small to warrant the attention of a qualified computer consultant?

We wrote this book because we want you, the SMB owner, to know that none of those reasons are good reasons to not protect your mission-critical business data. And the best news?

THANK YOU FOR READING

Protecting your network is less expensive than you think when you hire a qualified managed service provider.

If you have any questions about how managed services can help excel your business, we urge you to reach out to us at www.ITFreeFall.com. We'll be more than happy to answer any questions you have about our services and how they can improve your IT business processes.

Finally, we have a favor to ask. If you can spare a moment, please submit a review of IT Free Fall. Whether you loved it or hated it, we would love your feedback. www.ITFreeFall.com/Review

As you may already know, reviews can be difficult to come by these days. You, the reader, have the power to make or break a book. We hope you would feel confident recommending this book to others who may benefit from knowing a little more about small business IT support and service.

Photo by Creative Photography / Jeanne Hauser

Thanks again for taking the time to read
IT Free Fall.

Nick, Paul and

the Staff of

SNECS!

GLOSSARY OF TERMS

DON'T BE FOOLED BY "GEEK SPEAK"

Photo by David Goehring

GLOSSARY OF TERMS

Once you start working with a qualified consultant, you'll quickly start hearing terms that you may not be familiar with. Remember from earlier chapters that one of the marks of a good consultant is that they won't have a problem taking the time to explain these terms to you, but it still doesn't hurt to have a basic understanding of common IT terms. We've compiled a list of these terms and included plain English explanations of each to make it a little easier for you to communicate with your consultant on a technical level.

Please note: The list below is from the FCC Small Biz Cyber Planning Guide.

Adware

Any software application that displays advertising banners while the program is running. Adware often includes code that tracks a user's personal information and passes it on to third parties without the user's authorization or knowledge. And if you gather enough of it, adware slows down your computer significantly. Over time, performance can be so degraded that you may have trouble working productively. See also "Spyware" and "Malware."

Anti-Virus Software

Software designed to detect and potentially eliminate viruses before they have had a chance to wreak havoc on the system. Anti-virus software can also repair or quarantine files that have already been infected by virus activity. See also "Virus and Electronic Infections."

Application

Software that performs automated functions for a user, such as word processing, spreadsheets, graphics, presentations, and databases—as opposed to operating system (**OS**) software.

Attachment

A file that has been added to an email—often an image or document. It could be something useful for you or something harmful to your computer. See also "Virus."

Authentication

Confirming the correctness of the claimed identity of an individual user, machine, software component or any other entity.

Authorization

The approval, permission or empowerment for someone or something to do something.

Backdoor

Hidden software or hardware mechanism used to circumvent security controls.

GLOSSARY OF TERMS

Backup

File copies that are saved as protection against loss, damage or unavailability of the primary data. Saving methods include high-capacity tape, separate disk sub-systems or on the Internet. Off-site backup storage is ideal, sufficiently far away to reduce the risk of environmental damage such as flood, which might destroy both the primary and the backup if kept nearby.

Bandwidth

The capacity of a communication channel to pass data such as text, images, video or sound through the channel in a given amount of time. Usually expressed in bits per second.

Blacklisting Software

A form of filtering that blocks only websites specified as harmful. Parents and employers sometimes use such software to prevent children and employees from visiting certain websites. You can add and remove sites from the "not permitted" list. This method of filtering allows for more full use of the Internet but is less efficient at preventing access to any harmful material that is not on the list. See also "Whitelisting Software."

Blended Threat

A computer network attack that seeks to maximize the severity of damage and speed of contagion by combining methods—for example, using characteristics of both viruses and worms. See also "Electronic Infection."

Blog

Short for "Web log," a blog is usually defined as an online diary or journal. It is usually frequently updated and offered in a dated log format with the most recent entry at the top of the page. It often contains links to other websites along with commentary on those sites or specific subjects, such as politics, news, pop culture or computers.

Broadband

General term used to refer to high-speed network connections such as cable modem and Digital Subscriber Line (**DSL**). These types of "always on" Internet connections are actually more susceptible to some security threats than computers that access the Web via dial-up service.

Browser

A client software program that can retrieve and display information from servers on the World Wide Web. Often known as a "Web browser" or

"Internet browser." Examples include Microsoft's Internet Explorer, Google's Chrome, Apple's Safari, and Mozilla's Firefox.

Brute Force Attack

An exhaustive password-cracking procedure that tries all possibilities, one by one. See also "Dictionary Attack" and "Hybrid Attack."

Clear Desk Policy

A policy that directs all personnel to clear their desks at the end of each working day, and file everything appropriately. Desks should be cleared of all documents and papers, including the contents of the "in" and "out" trays —not simply for cleanliness, but also to ensure that sensitive papers and documents are not exposed to unauthorized persons outside of working hours.

Clear Screen Policy

A policy that directs all computer users to ensure that the contents of the screen are protected from prying eyes and opportunistic breaches of confidentially. Typically, the easiest means of compliance is to use a screen saver that engages either on request or after a specified short period of time. See also "Shoulder Surfing."

GLOSSARY OF TERMS

Cookie

A small file that is downloaded by some websites to store a packet of information on your browser. Companies and organizations use cookies to remember your login or registration identification, site preferences, pages viewed and online "shopping-cart" so that the next time you visit a site, your stored information can automatically be pulled up for you. A cookie is obviously convenient but also presents potential security issues. You can configure your browser to alert you whenever a cookie is being sent. You can refuse to accept all cookies or erase all cookies saved on your browser.

Cyberbullying

Sending or posting harmful, cruel, rude or threatening messages, or slanderous information, text or images using the Internet or other digital communication devices.

Denial of Service Attack

The prevention of authorized access to a system resource or the delaying of system operations and functions. Often this involves a cybercriminal generating a large volume of data requests. See also "Flooding."

GLOSSARY OF TERMS

Dictionary Attack

A password-cracking attack that tries all of the phrases or words in a dictionary. See also "Brute Force Attack" and "Hybrid Attack."

Digital Certificate

The electronic equivalent of an ID card that establishes your credentials when doing business or other transactions on the Web. It contains your name, a serial number, expiration dates, a copy of the certificate holder's public key (used for encrypting messages and digital signatures) and the digital signature of the certificate-issuing authority so that a recipient can verify that the certificate is real.

Domain Hijacking

An attack in which an attacker takes over a domain by first blocking access to the domain's DNS server and then putting his own server up in its place.

Domain Name System (DNS)

The DNS is the way that Internet domain names are located. A website's domain name is easier to remember than its Internet Protocol (IP) address.

GLOSSARY OF TERMS

Dumpster Diving

Recovering files, letters, memos, photographs, IDs, passwords, checks, account statements, credit card offers and more from garbage cans and recycling bins. This information can then be used to commit identity theft.

Electronic Infections

Often called "viruses," these malicious programs and codes harm your computer and compromise your privacy. In addition to the traditional viruses, other common types include worms and Trojan horses. They sometimes work in tandem to do maximum damage. See also "Blended Threat."

Encryption

A data security technique used to protect information from unauthorized inspection or alteration. Information is encoded so that it appears as a meaningless string of letters and symbols during delivery or transmission. Upon receipt, the information is decoded using an encryption key.

End User License Agreement (EULA)

A contract between you and your software's vendor or developer. Many times, the EULA is presented as a dialog box that appears the first time you open the software and forces you to check "I accept" before you can proceed. Before accepting, though, read through it and make sure you understand and are comfortable with the terms of the agreement. If the software's EULA is hard to understand or you can't find it, beware!

Evil Twins

A fake wireless Internet hot spot that looks like a legitimate service. When victims connect to the wireless network, a hacker can launch a spying attack on their transactions on the Internet, or just ask for credit card information in the standard pay-for-access deal. See also "Man-in-the-Middle Attacks."

File-Sharing Programs

Sometimes called peer-to-peer (**P2P**) programs, these allow many different users to access the same file at the same time. These programs are often used to upload illegally and download music and other software. Examples include Nodezilla, Morpheus, uTorrent, and Vuze.

Firewall

A hardware or software link in a network that inspects all data packets coming and going from a computer, permitting only those that are authorized to reach the other side.

GLOSSARY OF TERMS

Flooding

An attack that attempts to cause a failure to the security of a computer by providing more input, such as a large volume of data requests, than it can properly process. See also "Denial of Service Attack."

Hacker

An individual who attempts to break into a computer without authorization.

HTTPS

When used in the first part of a URL (e.g., HTTP://), this term specifies the use of hypertext transfer protocol (**HTTP**) enhanced by a security mechanism such as Secure Socket Layer (**SSL**). Always look for the HTTPS on the checkout or order form page when shopping online or when logging into a site and providing your username and password.

Hybrid Attack

Builds on other password-cracking attacks by adding numerals and symbols to dictionary words. See also "Dictionary Attack" and "Brute Force Attack."

GLOSSARY OF TERMS

Instant Messaging (IM)

A service that allows people to send and get messages almost instantly. To send messages using instant messaging you need to download an instant messaging program and know the instant messaging address of another person who uses the same IM program. See also "Spim."

IP (Internet Protocol) Address

A computer's inter-network address, written as a series of four 8-bit numbers separated by periods, such as 123.45.678.990. Every website has an IP Address, although finding a website is considerably easier to do when using its domain name instead. See also "Domain Name System (**DNS**)."

Internet Service Provider (ISP)

A company that provides internet access to customers.

Keystroke Logger

A specific type of electronic infection that records victims' keystrokes and sends them to an attacker. This can be done with either hardware or software. See also "Trojan Horse."

GLOSSARY OF TERMS

Malware

A generic term for a number of different types of malicious code. See also "Adware and Spyware."

Man-In-the-Middle Attack

Posing as an online bank or merchant, a cybercriminal allows a victim to sign in over a Secure Sockets Layer (SSL) connection. The attacker then logs onto the real server using the client's information and steals credit card numbers.

Monitoring Software

Software products that allow parents to monitor or track the websites or email messages that a child visits or reads. See also "Blacklisting Software" and "Whitelisting Software."

Network

Two or more computer systems that are grouped together to share information, software and hardware.

Operating System (OS)

Programs that manage all the basic functions and programs on a computer, such as allocating system resources, providing access and security controls, maintaining file systems and managing communications between end users and hardware devices. Examples include Microsoft's Windows, Apple's Macintosh and Red Hat's Linux.

Password

A secret sequence of characters that are used as a means of authentication to confirm your identity in a computer program or online.

Password Cracking

Password cracking is the process of attempting to guess passwords, given the password file information. See also "Brute Force Attacks," "Dictionary Attacks," and "Hybrid Attacks."

Password Sniffing

Passive wiretapping, usually on a local area network, to gain knowledge of passwords.

Patch

A patch is a small security update released by a software manufacturer to fix bugs in existing programs. Your computer's software programs and/or operating system may be configured to check automatically for patches, or you may need to periodically visit the manufacturers' websites to see if there have been any updates.

Peer-to-Peer (P2P) Programs

See File-Sharing Programs.

GLOSSARY OF TERMS

Phishing

Soliciting private information from customers or members of a business, bank or other organization in an attempt to fool them into divulging confidential personal and financial information. People are lured into sharing usernames, passwords, account information or credit card numbers, usually by an official-looking message in an email or a pop-up advertisement that urges them to act immediately, usually by clicking on a link provided. See also "Vishing."

Pharming

Redirecting visitors from a real website to a bogus one. A user enters what is believed to be a valid Web address and is unknowingly redirected to an illegitimate site that steals the user's personal information. On the spoofed site, criminals may mimic real transactions and harvest private information unknowingly shared by users. With this, the attacker can then access the real website and conduct transactions using the credentials of a valid user.

Router

A hardware device that connects two or more networks and routes incoming data packets to the appropriate network. Many Internet Service

Providers (ISPs) provide these devices to their customers, and they often contain firewall protections.

Script

A file containing active content -- for example, commands or instructions to be executed by the computer.

Shoulder Surfing

Looking over a person's shoulder to get confidential information. It is an effective way to get information in crowded places because it's relatively easy to stand next to someone and watch as they fill out a form, enter a PIN number at an ATM machine or type a password. Can also be done long-distance with the aid of binoculars or other vision- enhancing devices. To combat it, experts recommend that you shield paperwork or your keypad from view by using your body or cupping your hand. Also, be sure you password-protect your computer screen when you must leave it unattended, and clear your desk at the end of the day. See also "Clear Desk Policy" and "Clear Screen Policy."

Skimming

A high-tech method by which thieves capture your personal or account information from your credit card, driver's license or even passport using an electronic device called a "skimmer." Such devices can be purchased online for under $50. Your card is swiped through the skimmer and the information contained in the magnetic strip on the card is then read into and stored on the device or an attached computer. Skimming is predominantly a tactic used to perpetuate credit card fraud but is also gaining in popularity amongst identity thieves.

Social Engineering

A euphemism for non-technical or low-technology means—such as lies, impersonation, tricks, bribes, blackmail, and threats—used to attack information systems. Sometimes telemarketers or unethical employees employ such tactics.

Social Networking Websites

Sites specifically focused on the building and verifying of social networks for whatever purpose. Many social networking services are also blog hosting services. There are more than 300 known social networking websites, including Facebook, MySpace, Friendster, Xanga, Twitter, and Tumblr. Such sites enable users to create online profiles and post pictures and share personal data such as their contact information, hobbies, activities, and interests. The sites facilitate connecting with other users with similar interests, activities, and locations. Sites vary in who may view a user's profile—some have settings which may be changed so that profiles can be viewed only by "friends." See also "Blogs."

Spam

Unwanted, unsolicited email from someone you don't know. Often sent in an attempt to sell you something or get you to reveal personal information.

Spim

Unwanted, unsolicited instant messages from someone you don't know. Often sent in an attempt to sell you something or get you to reveal personal information.

Spoofing

Masquerading so that a trusted IP address is used instead of the true IP address. A technique used by hackers as a means of gaining access to a computer system.

Spyware

Software that uses your Internet connection to send personally identifiable information about you to a collecting device on the Internet. It is often packaged with software that you download voluntarily so that even if you remove the downloaded program later, the spyware may remain. See also "Adware" and "Malware."

SSL (Secure Socket Layer)

An encryption system that protects the privacy of data exchanged by a website and the individual user. Used by websites whose URLs begin with HTTPS instead of HTTP.

Trojan Horse

A computer program that appears to be beneficial or innocuous, but also has a hidden and potentially malicious function that evades security mechanisms. A "keystroke logger," which records victims' keystrokes and sends them to an attacker or remote-controlled "zombie computers" are examples of the damage that can be done by Trojan horses. See also "Electronic Infection."

URL

Abbreviation for "Uniform (or Universal) Resource Locator." A way of specifying the location of publicly available information on the Internet. Also known as a "Web address."

URL Obfuscation

Taking advantage of human error, some scammers use phishing emails to guide recipients to fraudulent sites with names very similar to established sites. They use a slight misspelling or other subtle difference in the URL, such as "monneybank.com" instead of "moneybank.com" to redirect users to share their personal information unknowingly.

Virus

A hidden, self-replicating section of computer software, usually malicious logic that propagates by infecting—i.e., inserting a copy of itself into and becoming part of -- another program. A virus cannot run by itself; it requires that its host program be run to make the virus active. Often sent through email attachments. Also see "Electronic Infection" and "Blended Threat."

Vishing

Soliciting private information from customers or members of a business, bank or other organization in an attempt to fool them into divulging confidential personal and financial information. People are lured into sharing usernames, passwords, account information or credit card numbers, usually by an official-looking message in an email or a pop-up advertisement that urges them to act immediately—but in a vishing scam, they are urged to call the phone number provided rather than clicking on a link. See also "Phishing."

GLOSSARY OF TERMS

Vulnerability

A flaw that allows someone to operate a computer system with authorization levels in excess of that which the system owner specifically granted.

Whitelisting Software

A form of filtering that only allows connections to a pre-approved list of sites that are considered useful and appropriate for children. Parents sometimes use such software to prevent children from visiting all but certain websites. You can add and remove sites from the "permitted" list. This method is extremely safe but only allows for extremely limited use of the Internet.

Worm

Originally an acronym for "Write once, read many times," a type of electronic infection that can run independently, can propagate a complete working version of itself onto other hosts on a network, and may consume computer resources destructively. Once this malicious software is on a computer, it scans the network for another machine with a specific security vulnerability. When it finds one, it exploits the weakness to copy itself to the new machine, and then the worm starts replicating from there, as well. See also "Electronic Infection" and "Blended Threat."

GLOSSARY OF TERMS

Zombie Computer

A remote-access Trojan horse installs hidden code that allows your computer to be controlled remotely. Digital thieves then use robot networks of thousands of zombie computers to carry out attacks on other people and cover up their tracks. Authorities have a harder time tracing criminals when they go through zombie computers

REFERENCES

1. http://www.zetta.net/blog/infographic-it-downtime-affects-midsized-enterprises/ (Aberdeen Group study)

2. (Ronni J. Colville and George Spafford Configuration Management for Virtual and Cloud Infrastructures) - See more at http://www.evolven.com/blog/downtime-outages-and-failures-understanding-their-true-costs.html#sthash.rIDuEPYC.dpuf

3. Richmond House Group

4. FCC Small Business Cybersecurity Planning Guide

5. Creative Photography By Jeanne Hauser www.hauserphoto.com

P.S.

Please visit www.ITFreeFall.com/Bonus for a bonus section where we will share with you a list of the **top 10** things every SMB owner <u>must ask</u> their current IT provider along with other great **bonus audio and video** material.

Made in the USA
Middletown, DE
12 June 2015